Introduction to Elizabethan Literature

Studies in Language and Literature

INTRODUCTION TO

Elizabethan
Literature

BY KENNETH MUIR

THE UNIVERSITY OF LIVERPOOL

RANDOM HOUSE   NEW YORK

Preface

This book does not pretend to be a history of Elizabethan literature. In the limited space at my disposal I have preferred to concentrate on the writers who have the most intrinsic interest, and especially on the poets and dramatists.

As I have written before on five or six of the authors of the period, I may inadvertently have echoed phrases from my previous treatment of them; and I have doubtless been influenced by the work of other critics and scholars, many of whom are listed at the end of each chapter. But I have reread most of the literature of the period and endeavored to judge it afresh.

I am indebted to my colleague, Mrs. Inga-Stina Ewbank, for reading with a critical eye the first draft of the book.

KENNETH MUIR

The University of Liverpool
March, 1967

Contents

Introduction to Elizabethan Literature

I
Introduction

Elizabeth I reigned for forty-five years (1558–1603); but most of the works that would be chosen by critic or general reader to exemplify "Elizabethan literature" were crowded into the second half of her reign. Indeed, all the best plays and novels, and most of the good poetry, were written after the defeat of the Spanish Armada in 1588. It is tempting to believe that the facts are causally connected and to ascribe the flowering of literature and music to the removal of the danger of invasion and to an upsurge of patriotic feeling. But it should be remembered that the Elizabethans themselves believed there would be another attempt at invasion; the sense of national identity was not new in 1588—it can be traced back to the reign of Henry VIII—but was intensified by the exploits of Elizabethan seamen, in battle, buccaneering, and discovery and by continuous propaganda on behalf of the Tudor monarchy.

The long misery of the Hundred Years' War and the greater misery of the Wars of the Roses, which brought feudalism to an end, made it easy for people to appreciate the comparative peace ushered in by the defeat of Richard III at Bosworth and the marriage of Henry VII to a Yorkist princess. There were rebellions in the reigns of Henry VII, Henry VIII, Mary, and Elizabeth, but they were easily crushed. The theme of Hall's chronicle—*The Union of the Two Noble and Illustre Families of Lancastre and York* (1550)—was precisely the advantages of the Tudor settlement after years of civil war; this was the theme of Daniel's *Civil Wars*; and, whatever ironies and reservations he may have had, this was also the theme of Shakespeare's histories.

The later rebellions in the Tudor period were inspired mostly by religious zeal; but in Elizabeth's reign the real danger to the Queen was from assassination by Catholics after she had been excommunicated. After the execution of Mary, Queen of Scots, who was implicated in one of the plots, the danger was appreciably less; and even if Spanish troops had been able to invade England in 1588, they would have had little or no support from Catholic fifth columnists.

The aim of the religious settlement at the beginning of the reign was outward conformity. Elizabeth had no wish to pry into men's souls, provided they attended church on Sundays. She wished to avoid the persecutions of the previous reigns and hoped that her middle by T. S. Eliot, in which he quoted some of the best passages. But the general level of the *Ten Tragedies* is deplorable, with the faults of excessive alliteration, lack of rhythmical skill, and bombastic diction. Only Jasper Heywood in some of the choruses comes near to writing poetry that can be read for pleasure.

Arthur Golding's translation of Ovid's *Metamorphoses* (1567) has also been overpraised, partly because it was a book that Shakespeare appears to have read with some care and enjoyment. Ezra Pound even went so far as to assert that Golding's translation was superior to *Paradise Lost*.[2] But unfortunately Golding, like many other translators of the period, chose the clumsiest of all verse forms, the rhymed fourteener, which inevitably breaks in the middle so that it has the jog-trot rhythm of ballad meter. One famous passage may be given, Medea's invocation, which Shakespeare was to transform into Prospero's farewell to his art:

Ye airs and winds, ye elves of hills, of brooks, of woods
   alone,
Of standing lakes, and of the night approach ye everyone;
Through help of whom (the crooked banks much wondering at the thing)
I have compelled streams to run clean backward to their
   spring.

It will be noticed that, apart from the metrical crudity, Golding is hampered by the difficulty of finding a rhyme.

If we turn to the drama, we find that the plays written for the professional stage before the advent of the University Wits deserved Sidney's ridicule (see pp. 130ff.);

[2] *Literary Essays,* ed. T. S. Eliot (New York: New Directions, 1953), p. 238n.

and even *Gorboduc,* written for performance by amateurs in 1561 by Thomas Norton and Thomas Sackville and, despite some reservations, praised by Sidney for "rising to the height of Seneca his style," is a somewhat dreary forerunner of the great age of drama. Apart from the rhymed choruses, which moralize on the action, the play is written in monotonous, end-stopped blank verse. The authors deserve the credit of transfering to the stage for the first time the medium that had previously been used only by Surrey in his translation of two books of the *Æneid*. Its didactic purpose was to point out the dangers of a disputed succession and, hence, to persuade the Queen to marry; but though Sidney asserted that the play succeeded in teaching delightfully, it has little to recommend it. Lifeless characters orate about the action, and there are few touches of poetry. This is odd, because Sackville (1536–1608) was the first Elizabethan poet to rise above mediocrity. To *The Mirror for Magistrates*—a collection of didactic poems by several hands, in which people who had fallen from greatness moralized tediously on their fates—he contributed a poem in which Buckingham described his fall, together with a splendid induction. These contributions, published in 1563, have none of the weaknesses of *Gorboduc*. Some idea of Sackville's quality can be gauged from two of the opening stanzas:

> The wrathful winter 'proaching on apace,
> With blustring blasts had all ybared the treen,
> And old Saturnus with his frosty face
> With chilling cold had pierced the tender green:
> The mantles rent, wherein enwrapped been
> The gladsome groves that now lay overthrown;
> The tapets torn, and every bloom down blown.

Hawthorn had lost his motley livery,
The naked twigs were shivering all for cold:
And dropping down the tears abundantly
Each thing, methought, with weeping eye me told
The cruel season, bidding me withhold
Myself within, for I was gotten out
Into the fields whereas I walked about.

This leads to a description of Hades so magnificent that it is difficult to understand why *Gorboduc* is so flat and why Sackville wrote or published no more verse, even though he became involved in public affairs.

Sackville was an amateur, and, like many courtiers, he may have felt that publication of verse in the normal way was beneath his dignity. We have lost a good deal of fine poetry, by Ralegh and others, because of what has been called "the stigma of print." George Gascoigne (1535?–77) was a courtier too, but more of a professional, and his pioneering work has sometimes been undervalued, perhaps because he tried his hand at so many different kinds of literature—drama, fiction, poetry, and reportage. Both his plays were translations from the Italian. *Supposes* (1573), a version of a famous comedy by Ariosto, *Gli Suppositi,* is written in well-turned, speakable prose. It is chiefly famous as the source of the underplot of *The Taming of the Shrew,* but it is much more accomplished than any other comedy of this early period. It provided a model that other dramatists were slow to imitate, Spenser's nine comedies not having survived.

Gascoigne's tale, "The Adventures of Master F. J." (1573), is a lively narrative—"the first prose tale of modern life"—probably based on fact, and he also described *The Spoil of Antwerp* (1577). His longer poems,

The Steel Glass (1576) and *The Complaint of Phylo-
mene* (1576), are interesting as forerunners of Spenser;
but the former has avowed affinities with Langland, and
the latter exhibits the influence of Chaucer, which saved
Gascoigne from the faults of the poetasters of his generation:

> In sweet April, the messenger to May,
> When honey drops do melt in golden showers,
> When every bird records her lover's lay,
> And western winds do foster forth our flowers,
> Late in an even I walked out alone
> To hear the descant of the Nightingale,
> And as I stood, I heard her make great moan,
> Waymenting much, and thus she told her tale.

The diction is simple and unaffected, the versification
smooth; and at the date the poem was written these
virtues were rare. But Gascoigne's longer poems are, on
the whole, less successful than the shorter lyrics con-
tained in *A Hundreth Sundry Flowers* (1573) and
Posies (1575). One of the best is entitled "Gascoigne's
Lullaby," which begins:

> Sing lullabie, as women do
> Wherewith they bring their babes to rest;
> And lullabie can I sing too,
> As womanly as can the best.
> With lullabie they still the child,
> And if I be not much beguiled,
> Full many wanton babes have I
> Which must be stilled with lullabie.

He proceeds to sing a lullaby to his youth, his gazing
eyes, and his wanton will. It is a charming application
of a form of popular poetry.

Gascoigne died in 1577; and two years later Spenser's

poetry was introduced to the world with the publication
of *The Shepherd's Calendar*. The great age had begun;
but as Nashe said of Gascoigne, "he first beat the path
to that perfection which our best poets have aspired to
since his departure."

Suggested Reading

Tottel's *Songs and Sonnets, The Paradise of Dainty Devices, A Gorgeous Gallery of Gallant Inventions,* and *A
Handful of Pleasant Delights* have all been edited by H. E.
Rollins (Cambridge, Mass.: Harvard Univ. Press, 1924–29).
Seneca's *Tenne Tragedies* have been reprinted with an introduction by T. S. Eliot (New York: Alfred A. Knopf,
1927). Golding's translation of Ovid's *Metamorphoses* has
recently been edited by J. F. Nims (New York: Macmillan,
1966). *The Mirror for Magistrates* has been splendidly edited
by Lily B. Campbell (San Marino, Calif.: Huntington Library, 1938). *Thomas Sackville* by P. Bacquet (Geneva: Droz,
1966) is admirable. Gascoigne's *Works* were edited by J. W.
Cunliffe (Cambridge Univ. Press, 1907–10). See also *George
Gascoigne, Elizabethan Courtier, Soldier, and Poet* by C. T.
Prouty (New York: Blom, 1942).

II
Edmund Spenser

Edmund Spenser (1552–99) was born in London, his "most kindly nurse." He was educated under the enlightened Mulcaster at Merchant Taylors School, and later at Pembroke College, Cambridge, where he obtained his M.A. in 1576. A year or two later he was introduced by Gabriel Harvey, a fellow of Pembroke College, to Sir Philip Sidney. Spenser had published some verse translations while he was still at school; and before he met Sidney he was writing verses about his love for "Rosalind"; but it was doubtless Sidney's encouragement that led to the completion and publication of *The Shepherd's Calendar* in 1579. He had written a large number of other poems by this time; a few were absorbed into later works, but most of them have not survived. He had also written nine comedies in prose, which Harvey apparently preferred to some early specimens of *The Faerie Queene.*

The Areopagus—the name Spenser gave to the trio of poets, himself, Sidney, and Dyer—experimented in classical meters and proclaimed for a while "a general surceasing and silence of bald rhymers"; and they were encouraged by Harvey in this abortive enterprise. It was partly caused by the comparative dearth of good English poetry during the early years of Elizabeth's reign; and it was abandoned as soon as the poets realized that they could themselves write good poems in rhymed verse.

Sidney and Spenser wanted to do for English poetry what Marot, Ronsard, and Du Bellay had done for French poetry; and Spenser wished to emulate and even "overgo" Ariosto. How successful they were in their aims can be seen not merely by consideration of the works of Spenser and Sidney, but by comparing the early Elizabethan miscellanies, such as *A Gorgeous Gallery of Gallant Inventions,* with *The Phoenix Nest* or *England's Helicon,* which show much greater technical skill.

Spenser was following the precedent of Virgil and Petrarch in coming before the world first with his eclogues; but he and his friends did everything to ensure the success of the volume. It was dedicated to Sidney; it was provided with explanatory notes by E. K., as though the book already had classic status; and the same Kirke also provided a prefatory letter to Harvey. At the same time Spenser concealed himself behind the pseudonym of Immerito, and in the poems themselves he appears as Colin Clout. In the introductory verses he pretends his book was "base begot with blame"; but in the epilogue he echoes the boast of Horace and Ovid:

Lo! I have made a calendar for every year,
That steel in strength, and time in durance shall outwear.

Spenser's public relations officers did their work well. The book immediately established Spenser's reputation, and Sidney in his *Defence of Poesy* singled it out for special praise.

Yet much of it, in the light of Spenser's later achievement, is of little importance. Some of the eclogues are concerned with the state of the church (May, July, September), and these have inevitably dated. Others express Colin Clout's love for Rosalind (January, June). There is the usual competition between shepherds (August) as in Virgil's seventh eclogue. Spenser provides a skillful imitation of a Marot elegy (November), but the song in praise of Queen Elizabeth (April) is the only poem that gives promise of Spenser's future greatness, more for its technical skill than for its imaginative power. These are the first two stanzas:

Ye dainty Nymphs, that in this blessed brook
        Do bathe your breast,
Forsake your wat'ry bowers, and hither look
        At my request:
And eke you virgins that on Parnasse dwell,
Whence floweth Helicon, the learned well,
        Help me to blaze
        Her worthy praise,
Which in her sex doth all excell.

Of fair Elisa be your silver song,
        That blessed wight;

The flower of Virgins, may she flourish long
    In princely plight.
For she is Syrinx' daughter without spot,
Which Pan, the shepherds' god, of her begot:
    So sprung her grace
    Of heavenly race,
No mortal blemish may her blot.

Spenser obtained a post in Ireland and remained there
for nine years working on *The Faerie Queene*. Three
books were completed by 1589, and he came to London
accompanied by Ralegh, who presented him at court.
He received permission from the Queen to dedicate the
poem to her. The first three books were published in
1590; and before he returned to Ireland in the following
year, disappointed of his hopes of advancement at court,
Spenser left with the printer a volume of *Complaints,*
consisting mostly of early work. The translations of tedious allegorical sonnets by Petrarch and Du Bellay are
undistinguished, though by such imitations Spenser
gradually attained a style of his own. Here and there
the formal laments rise into poetry, as in the lines on
Leicester in "The Ruins of Time":

O trustless state of miserable men,
That build your bliss on hope of earthly thing,
And vainly think yourselves half happy then,
When painted faces with smooth flattering
Do fawn on you, and your wide praises sing,
And when the courting masker louteth low,
Him true in heart and trusty to you trow.

The best things in the volume are "Mother Hubberd's
Tale," an allegorical account of Spenser's disillusionment with the court, and a gay and exquisite trifle,
"Muiopotmos," which has some fine passages of description.

As soon as he got back to his Irish estate, Spenser wrote a thinly veiled account of his visit to London, under the title *Colin Clout's Come Home Again*. In the second half of the poem Colin Clout describes his disillusionment with court life, though not, of course, with the Queen. Spenser would gladly have escaped from what he regarded as his exile in Ireland, although advancement at court might have left him less time to proceed with the composition of *The Faerie Queene*. *Colin Clout's Come Home Again* is written in a familiar style, easy, graceful, and colloquial, in such a way that this fragment of autobiography is touched with poetry and a quiet humor, as well as by a moral distaste for the arts required for success:

> For, sooth to say, it is no sort of life
> For shepherd fit to lead in that same place
> Where each one seeks, with malice and with strife,
> To thrust down other into foul disgrace,
> Himself to raise: and he doth soonest rise
> That best can handle his deceitful wit
> In subtle shifts, and finest sleights devise,
> Either by slandering his well-deemed name
> Through leasings lewd and feigned forgery,
> Or else by breeding him some blot of blame
> By creeping close into his secrecy;
> To which him needs a guileful hollow heart,
> Masked with fair dissembling courtesy,
> A filed tongue furnished with terms of art—
> No art of school, but courtier's schoolery.
> For arts of school have there small countenance,
> Counted but toys to busy idle brains,
> And there professors find small maintenance,
> But to be instruments of others' gains.

The poem was not published until 1595; and in the same year appeared Spenser's sonnet sequence, *Amoretti,* along with *Epithalamion,* the poem that celebrates his

marriage to Elizabeth Boyle. The sonnets were composed over a number of years, addressed originally, it
is supposed, to more than one woman. Many of them
were suggested by Italian and French sonneteers—
Petrarch, Desportes, Du Bellay—although none is a
translation. They lack the force and reality of Sidney's
and Shakespeare's, and the sequence is without narrative interest; but they are, with the exception of Shakespeare's, the most melodious of all Elizabethan sonnets.
The form Spenser adopted was a compromise between
the Italian and the Shakespearian: he kept the final
couplet, as Shakespeare was to do, but he linked the
quatrains together by giving the first and second, and
the second and third, a common rhyme. This gives a
greater unity to the sonnets; and many of them, despite
the lack of originality and passion, are nicely turned
and beautifully phrased. Like most Elizabethan sonneteers, Spenser combined fact with fiction, imitation
with personal feeling. We cannot be certain in any particular sonnet whether fact or fiction predominates. One
of them refers to the completion of six books of *The
Faerie Queene*:

> After so long a race as I have run
> Through fairyland, which those six books compile,

and praises his betrothed for being

> Fit for the handmaid of the Faery Queen.

In another sonnet the poet promises to immortalize his
lady, but we cannot assume that it records an actual
incident in his courtship:

> One day I wrote her name upon the strand,
> But came the waves and washed it away:
> Again I wrote it with a second hand,

But came the tide, and made my pains his prey.
"Vain man", said she, "thou dost in vain assay
A mortal thing so to immortalize,
For I myself shall like to this decay,
And eke my name be wiped out likewise."
"Not so", quod I, "let baser things devise
To die in dust, but you shall live by fame:
My verse your virtues rare shall eternize,
And in the heavens write your glorious name:
Where, whereas death shall all the world subdue,
Our love shall live, and later life renew."

We do not obtain a clear picture of Elizabeth Boyle
—or of any other recipient—from reading the sonnets,
but only of Spenser's feelings and his reading. She has
an angel's face; she is like pearls and rubies; she is
chaste as ice; and her hair is golden. In his imagery
Spenser makes copious use of the better-known stories
of classical mythology—Venus, Daphne, Arion, Or-
pheus, Cupid, Narcissus, Pandora, and Penelope—and
of second-hand natural history. It is unlikely that
Spenser ever saw the lion, the panther, and the tiger
he uses for his similes. Even his flowers are mostly em-
blematic, rather than derived from observation.

Epithalamion is another matter. It is Spenser's most
perfect poem and one of the most beautiful in the language. Its model is the *canzone* of Petrarch, who used
a similar mixture of long and short lines and a similar
rhyme scheme. Spenser was such a careful and scrupulous
artist that one is bound to inquire the reason for the
poem's irregularities, why one stanza has 17 lines instead
of the normal 18, why the refrain is altered in the last
eight stanzas. In *Short Time's Endless Monument*
(1960) A. K. Hieatt suggests that if one subtracts the
68 short lines, one is left with 365, the number of days

in the year. With the envoy, there are twenty-four stanzas, the number of hours in the day. Spenser's marriage was on the shortest day, when there are eight hours of darkness, so the refrain changes in the last eight stanzas. This ingenuity is not important in itself, but it illustrates the deliberate art with which the poem was composed.

The form is Italian, but Spenser goes back to Catullus for the general structure of the poem. He writes within a tradition, but since he is writing of his own wedding, he irradiates the conventions with personal feeling. He blends Roman paganism with English Christianity, classical mythology with Irish landscape, the love of art with the art of love.

At the beginning of the poem, Spenser asks Hymen with his procession of torchbearers to awaken his bride; he calls the bridesmaids "nymphs"; the people shout, "Io Hymen," as they did in Roman times; the three handmaids of Venus prepare the bride, who is

> Like unto Maia, when as Jove her took,
> In Tempe, lying on the flow'ry grass
> Twixt sleep and wake, after she weary was
> With bathing in the Acidalian brook;

the moon appears as Diana; and Spenser prays to Juno and Hebe. But the actual wedding ceremony is a Christian one, and there are echoes from the Song of Songs and the Psalms. There are also reminiscences of English folklore:

> Ne let the Pouke, nor other evil sprites,
> Ne let mischievous witches with their charms,
> Ne let hobgoblins, names whose sense we see not,
> Fray us with things that be not.

Despite the mingling of apparently incompatible traditions, we are not troubled by any sense of incongruity. Spenser unifies them by the power of his imagination, which acts as a solvent to his learning, by his sensuous delight in beauty, and by his love, which is both passionate and spiritualized.

The companion poem, *Prothalamion* (1596), written to celebrate the betrothals of Elizabeth and Katharine Somerset, is more relaxed and less unified than *Epithalamion*. But a kind of unity is achieved by making the swans symbolize the brides, who were to be married from Essex House; and this enabled Spenser to mention various buildings on the banks of the Thames and to pay tribute to the Earl of Essex, then at the height of his popularity, who had recently returned from his Cádiz expedition:

> Yet therein now doth lodge a noble Peer,
> Great England's glory and the world's wide wonder,
> Whose dreadful name late through all Spain did thunder,
> And Hercules' two pillars standing near
> Did make to quake and fear:
> Fair branch of Honour, flower of Chivalry,
> That fillest England with thy triumph's fame,
> Joy have thou of thy noble victory.

In the same year Spenser published *Four Hymns*. He states in the epistle dedicatory that the first two, to Love and Beauty, were written "in the greener times" of his youth and that he had added the hymns to Heavenly Love and Heavenly Beauty by way of retraction. There was, in fact, nothing to retract, but rather to complement. The four poems are not among Spenser's best, but they are nevertheless interesting for the light they throw on his ideas at the time he was engaged in writing *The*

Faerie Queene. In the first hymn, in praise of Cupid, there is some ambivalence. Spenser spends many of his thirty-one stanzas in describing the pains of unreturned love, which seem to be only partly compensated by the brave exploits undertaken by the lover in his attempts to win the favor of his lady, and by the belief that, if she should ever relent, the woes he has suffered would seem a small penance for a great reward. These ideas were a commonplace of Italian poetry. One of Petrarch's best-known poems, translated by Wyatt,[1] is a debate on whether the pains of love are compensated by its power to inspire to noble deeds. Although Spenser had certainly read some of the Neoplatonists, he makes only a casual use of their doctrines. The second hymn, in praise of Beauty, is addressed to Venus; and in it Spenser distinguishes between the rosy lips and cheeks, which are subject to decay, and the inward beauty of the soul, even though a beautiful appearance is the outward and visible sign of a "beauteous soul." True lovers tend to idealize the qualities of the beloved, but that is because

> Lovers' eyes more sharply sighted be
> Than other men's, and in dear love's delight
> See more than any other eyes can see.

Berowne's defense of love in *Love's Labour's Lost,* written at about the same time as Spenser's poem, uses independently some of the same ideas; but *Troilus and Cressida,* in its attack on idealization, seems almost a rebuttal of them.

The third hymn, on Heavenly Love, consists simply of

---

[1] *Collected Poems of Sir Thomas Wyatt,* ed. K. Muir (Cambridge, Mass.: Harvard Univ. Press, 1949), No. 8.

an account of the redemption of man by Jesus Christ;
and the fourth hymn, on Heavenly Beauty, approaches
the subject by gradual stages, through Platonic ideas,
cherubim and seraphim, to Sapience,

The sovereign darling of the Deity,

who kindles the love of God in man. This was probably
Spenser's last poem, and it may account for his apparent
difficulty in continuing *The Faerie Queene*. The fragment he did write—the *Mutability Cantos* (published
in 1609)—is close in spirit to the third and fourth
hymns.

Spenser's original intention had been to write an epic
in twelve books, but it is not certain that he continued
with his plan after the publication of the second install-
ment in 1596. The specter of the long poem haunted the
poets of the Renaissance, and even as late as the nineteenth century Tennyson was constrained to write his
pseudo-epic, *Idylls of the King*. When Spenser began
his poem, in 1580 or before, he had taken Ariosto's
Orlando Furioso as his model, a poem published half a
century before, which Sir John Harrington was later to
translate. Tasso's *Gerusalemme Liberata* appeared just in
time for Spenser to be influenced by it. The two Italian
epics differ considerably from those of Homer and Virgil.
Unlike the classical epics, they have multiple plots, ingeniously interwoven, and they are written in stanza
form; but they also differ from each other. Whereas
Ariosto's has a great variety of tone, from "a Virgilian
grandeur and pathos" to frank bawdiness reminiscent of
some of *The Canterbury Tales,* Tasso's, whose theme is
the First Crusade, has a greater unity of tone, a con-

tinuous high seriousness. In spite of Spenser's Protestant-
ism, the bent of his mind was closer to Tasso's Catholi-
cism, tinged with the ideas of the Counter Reformation,
than it was to the undidactic aestheticism. of Ariosto.

The middle books of *The Faerie Queene,* in which the
influence of Ariosto is most apparent and in which there
are a large number of loosely related episodes, were
probably written first; and it was probably parts of these
that Harvey read and criticized. There is little real allegory in Ariosto; and although Spenser uses plenty of
allegory in these books, they differ from Book I, in which
there is a single story and a sustained allegory.

During the fifteen years in which Spenser was working on the poem, his plan was considerably modified,
perhaps more than once; and when, as late as 1589, he
wrote a letter to Ralegh to explain the structure and
allegory, it is difficult to believe that this describes the
plan with which he started and quite impossible to believe that the six books correspond with it. He tells
Ralegh that the poem is "a continued allegory, or dark
conceit," that its main purpose is "to fashion a gentle-
man or noble person in virtuous and gentle discipline,"
that Prince Arthur "is perfected in the twelve private
moral virtues, as Aristotle hath devised," and that these
twelve virtues are separately embodied in the twelve
knights who give their names to the different books.
Arthur, having seen the Fairy Queen in a vision, goes in
quest of her; and he makes a brief appearance in each
of the six completed books. In Book XII Spenser intended to describe the annual feast of the Fairy Queen
and the start of the twelve adventures recorded earlier.

When and how Arthur was to meet the Fairy Queen

Spenser does not explain, nor how he could deal with twelve virtues if the twelfth book was to be wholly devoted to the annual feast. Holiness, moreover, is not an Aristotelian virtue, and Aristotle does not enumerate twelve private virtues. It is obvious that Spenser had not planned the whole poem in every detail and that he modified his original conception as he wrote. The function of the letter to Ralegh was simply to give some idea to the readers of the first three books how they were related to the whole; but Spenser's plan was not rigid, and in some respects it was deliberately vague.

The general moral allegory represented by the virtues featured in the various books is the most important kind used by Spenser; but this does not mean that we can say that Sir Guyon equals Temperance and that Britomart equals Chastity, but rather that the books in which they appear set forth the desirability of those virtues.

The second kind of allegory is topical. Duessa, for example, represents Mary, Queen of Scots; Belphoebe, Elizabeth; Timias, Ralegh. This topical allegory must obviously have been more interesting to Spenser's original readers than it can be to us.

There is a third kind of allegory in the poem, exemplified by the pageant of the Seven Deadly Sins in Book I and by the Cave of Mammon in Book II. Such allegory called forth Spenser's powers of description, and it is as effective now as it was in the sixteenth century.

The fourth type of allegory, and the least important, is the introduction of minor characters with allegorical names. Sansfoy, Sansloy, and Sansjoy—representing Atheism, Lawlessness, and Joylessness—have only a minor rôle to play in the story, and Spenser takes small pains to characterize them.

It is important to realize that the allegory shifts frequently from one kind to another and that a character may be topically significant in one episode and morally significant elsewhere. Duessa, for example, is sometimes Mary, Queen of Scots, sometimes the Roman Catholic Church, and sometimes, more abstractly, Falsehood. The Fairy Queen herself signifies Glory as well as Queen Elizabeth. To a modern reader the topical allegory is generally of little importance, and scholars have, perhaps, spent too much time in trying to find a contemporary of Spenser's to correspond with every character in the poem. A. C. Hamilton is surely right when he argues that Spenser was not trying to conceal his meaning, that he was expressing an image, rather than moral ideas, and that we should accept the primary meaning of the fable before searching for allegorical significances that are secondary in importance.

This does not mean, of course, that *The Faerie Queene* is not didactic. Milton declared that Spenser was a better teacher than Scotus or Aquinas, implying not that what he taught was better, but that he taught delightfully, and therefore more effectively. His method is similar to that of Sidney in *Arcadia*. He shows us heroes encountering temptations of various kinds; he presents us with hypocrites acting hypocritically and lechers behaving lecherously; he distinguishes the sensual from the sensuous, and true love from its various perversions. The characters, quite properly, are two-dimensional, flat, and typical. In Hamlet's words, Spenser shows "virtue her own feature, scorn her own image, and the very age and body of the time his form and pressure."

The poem should not be read, as Hazlitt and others have pretended, as though the meaning did not matter.

This would be to reduce the importance of the poem and misunderstand the nature of Spenser's art. But, on the other hand, we should not read the poem as an elaborate puzzle in which the story is merely a camouflage for the allegorical meaning. The inner meaning comes through, but it does not replace, the straightforward meaning of the narrative. Much of Spenser's meaning can be understood by a child, though the whole meaning will not be exhausted by a child's understanding.

In Book I, for example, the Redcross Knight, representing Holiness, accompanied by Una (or Truth), encounters in the wood the serpent Error. From the fact that "Her vomit full of books and papers was," we can deduce that Spenser was referring to doctrinal error or heresy. Later, Archimagus (or Hypocrisy) separates the Redcross Knight from Una (Holiness from Truth); and forthwith he meets with Sansfoy and Duessa (or Falsehood). We hardly need to know the allegorical equivalents of the characters, and still less the contemporary figures they may represent, to follow Spenser's meaning. The later cantos of Book I are equally plain.

Book II opens with the suicide of Amavia after the murder of her husband by Acrasia. She leaves behind her an infant stained with her blood, symbolizing humanity stained with original sin. The task of Sir Guyon is to destroy Acrasia's Bower of Bliss and so avenge the deaths of Amavia and her husband. The Bower of Bliss has to be a genuine temptation. Although Spenser doubtless intended the artificiality and perversities of the pleasures of the Bower to be contrasted with the natural and healthy delights of the Gardens of Adonis in Book III, some critics have suggested that the poet's imaginative sympathies conflicted with his didactic purpose. But, of course, unless the temptations were made alluring to the reader, we should not think that the hero who resisted them displayed any great fortitude. Acrasia is a witch; and the pleasures she offers, the attraction of which is conveyed to us by the enchanting poetry in which Spenser describes them, are designed to make men forget their knightly quests. Sir Guyon (or Temperance) captures Acrasia in a net and destroys the Bower; and the Palmer, who accompanies the Knight, draws the moral: The man who gives himself up to sensuality becomes a beast. We are shown how Acrasia's victims, like the rout in Milton's *Comus,* have been metamorphosed into wild beasts.

The third book is devoted to Chastity, and its central character is Britomart. Any poet depicting this virtue in the reign of the Virgin Queen was bound to have her in mind; but Spenser makes it clear in the introductory verses that although he is shadowing Elizabeth in "coloured shows" as the Fairy Queen and as Belphoebe, he does not presume to depict her. From his description of the Gardens of Adonis in this book, Spenser shows that his conception of chastity is neither sterile nor life-denying. The Gardens, which are contrasted with the Bower of Bliss, are not a place of sensuality for its own sake, but of generation and fecundity and of the love that leads to the continuance not merely of man, but of all living things:

> In that same garden all the goodly flowers
> Wherewith Dame Nature doth her beautify,
> And decks the garlands of her paramours,
> Are fetched: there is the first seminary
> Of all things that are born to live and die
> According to their kinds.

The Gardens are like Eden before the Fall, and, as Professor Graham Hough points out, the Venus "who presides over *The Faerie Queene*," whatever affinities she may have to the Uranian Venus, "goddess of love's delight, is also the Lucretian Venus" invoked in the opening lines of *De rerum natura*. The union of Venus and Adonis symbolizes the natural cycle of birth and death and rebirth; and it is only in the cantos of Book VII that Spenser contrasts this mutability with the unchangeable nature of God.

A book concerned with chastity is inevitably concerned also with its opposite. The story of the false Florimel, created by a witch, exemplifies the blinding effects of passion; and the episode of Hellenore among the satyrs shows the antithesis of chastity and the degrading effect of jealousy. More significant, perhaps, are the descriptions of the House of Busirane and the Mask of Cupid. C. S. Lewis argued in *The Allegory of Love* that Busirane is a symbol of courtly love, the extramarital cult of the Middle Ages. To other critics Busirane is rather a symbol of sexual love when it is treated as an end in itself, the chief end of existence. In Cupid's pageant, Shakespeare tells us in *Troilus and Cressida*, there is presented no monster; but Spenser gives a dismal catalogue of Cupid's train: Fancy (i.e., romantic love), Desire, Doubt, Danger, Fear, Hope, Suspicion, Grief, Fury, Displeasure, Pleasaunce, Despite, and Cruelty. Cupid himself is followed by others:

> Behind him was Reproach, Repentance, Shame;
> Reproach the first, Shame next, Repent behind;
> Repentance feeble, sorrowful, and lame,
> Reproach despiteful, careless and unkind,
> Shame most ill-favoured, bestial and blind:

> Shame loured, Repentance sighed, Reproach did scold;
> Reproach sharp stings, Repentance whips entwined,
> Shame burning brand-irons in her hand did hold:
> All three to each unlike, yet all made in one mould.

> And after them a rude confused rout
> Of persons flocked, whose names is hard to read:
> Amongst them was stern Strife, and Anger stout,
> Unquiet Care, and fond Unthriftyhead,
> Lewd Loss of Time, and Sorrow seeming dead,
> Inconstant Change, and false Disloyalty,
> Consuming Riotise, and guilty Dread
> Of heavenly vengeance, faint Infirmity,
> Vile Poverty, and lastly Death with infamy.

This long list of personifications, not fully realized, perhaps, clearly implies that sexual love becomes a curse if it is pursued obsessively; and elsewhere in this book we learn that even true lovers, like Amoret, may find that "the path of true love never did run smooth."

The evils of enslavement to passion are displayed in the previous canto. Cupid, blindfold, is the conqueror of the gods themselves and the ruin of many famous warriors:

> And all about the glistring walls were hung
> With warlike spoils and with victorious preys
> Of mighty conquerors and captains strong
> Which were whilome captived in their days
> To cruel love, and wrought their own decays:
> Their swords and spears were broke, and hauberques rent;
> And their proud garlands of triumphant bays
> Trodden in dust with fury insolent,
> To show the victor's might and merciless intent.

The remaining three books must be dismissed more briefly. Book IV is concerned with Friendship, a subject that is illustrated in a number of different stories.

Book V deals with Justice, and Spenser introduces some topical allegory about the rebellion in Ireland and the war in the Netherlands. Book VI, concerned with Courtesy, describes the task of Sir Calidore, who is thought to represent Sidney, of binding the Blatant Beast. Why Sidney should have the task of suppressing scandal is not clear. In Canto 10 of this book Spenser introduces himself into the story. When the three Graces and his own bride dance to his melody, the incident appears to be an allegorical presentation of the writing of *Epithalamion*.

There are weak passages in *The Faerie Queene,* episodes in which Spenser's imagination was not fully engaged, stanzas that are flat and prosaic, and others in which the allegory seems to be perfunctory. Before he reached the end of Book VI Spenser seems to have become oppressed with the magnitude of his task, which he could not hope to complete in less than six years. Even if he were to finish Book XII, the early books would have to be revised to make them consistent with the later ones; and, after that, there was his project of writing yet another twelve books to deal with the public virtues.

But in spite of the unfinished state of *The Faerie Queene,* and in spite of weaknesses here and there, the general level of the poetry is astonishingly high. The stanza invented by Spenser, to which his name is given, consisting of eight pentameters and a final alexandrine, is beautifully adapted to his purpose. The effect of the long last line is to make the reader treat each stanza as a separate unit, linked to those that precede and follow it, but self-contained. This slows the action and enables the reader to relish individual felicities and subtleties. The alexandrine enabled Spenser to avoid the epigram-

matic effect of a concluding couplet; and in most of the
stanzas there is a subtle interweaving of assonance and
alliteration. Here, for example, is one stanza describing
the Cave of Mammon:

> Both roof and floor and walls were all of gold,
> But overgrown with dust and old decay,
> And hid in darkness, that none could behold
> The hue thereof; for view of cheerful day
> Did never in that house itself display,
> But a faint shadow of uncertain light,
> Such as a lamp, whose life does fade away,
> Or as the Moon, clothed with cloudy night,
> Does show to him that walks in fear and sad affright.

Apart from the obvious alliteration (e.g., the repetition
of *d* in ll. 2–4, of *l* in ll. 6 and 7, of *c* in l. 8, and *s* and
f in l. 9), "walls" in the first line is echoed by "all," and
"hue" in l. 4 is echoed by "view," and the *v* of "view" is
repeated internally in "never" in the next line. Wordsworth's "Guilt and Sorrow," Byron's *Childe Harold's
Pilgrimage,* and Shelley's *The Revolt of Islam* and *Ado-
nais* were all written in the Spenserian stanza; but only
Keats in "The Eve of St. Agnes" approached Spenser
in richness of texture and delicacy of sound effects.

Although Spenser introduces a large number of archaic
words, the general effect is not one of artificiality. It is
noteworthy that Wordsworth and Coleridge, reacting as
they did against the poetic diction of the eighteenth century, had nothing but admiration for Spenser's. Coleridge,
indeed, declared that there was no poet "whose writings
would safelier stand the test" of Wordsworth's theory
of poetic diction than Spenser's; and *The Faerie Queene*
was "preeminently dear" to Wordsworth.[2]

---

[2] Coleridge, *Biographia Literaria* (1817), Chapter XVIII; Wordsworth's poem "Personal Talk."

Spenser was in some respects the heir of the Middle Ages, but he was also a typical product of the Renaissance. He united in his work the diverse strains he derived from Chaucer, the Pléiade, Ariosto, and Tasso. He combined a sensuous delight in the beauty of art and nature with the ideas he took from the Neoplatonists; a passionate involvement in the political issues of his time with a deep, and almost puritanical, religious sense; a lifelong devotion to his art with a conviction that it should be used to influence both the views and the conduct of his readers.

When he began to write, Elizabethan poetry was essentially minor: it was lacking in craftsmanship, weak in imagery, cliché-ridden, and provincial. When he died, his example, and that of Sidney, had raised the general level of verse so that even the poetasters had learned how to construct a poem and how to write smooth and musical lines. His influence was, indeed, so pervasive that the metaphysical poets reacted against it.

Spenser has been called the poets' poet because he has been most appreciated by his peers. His influence on Daniel and Drayton and on the Spenserians in the first half of the seventeenth century is apparent. He was Milton's chief master; and although in the eighteenth century it was the minor poets who found in him an escape from the prevailing style, during the period of the romantic revival he again became a liberating force. During the present century, the rediscovery of the metaphysicals and the questioning of Milton's supremacy led to a corresponding devaluation of Spenser's work, but he has never lacked enthusiastic admirers.

Suggested Reading

The best and most elaborate edition of Spenser's works is the Variorum, edited by E. Greenlaw, C. G. Osgood, and others (Baltimore: Johns Hopkins Press, 1932–49). The best inexpensive edition is edited by E. de Sélincourt (Oxford Univ. Press, 1912). Among the numerous books on Spenser published in recent years, the following may be mentioned:

Edmund Spenser, by W. L. Renwick (London: Arnold, 1925).

The Poetry of Edmund Spenser, by W. Nelson (New York: Columbia Univ. Press, 1963).

The Structure of Allegory in The Faerie Queene, by A. C. Hamilton (Oxford: Clarendon Press, 1961).

A Preface to The Faerie Queene, by G. Hough (London: Duckworth, 1962).

III
Sir Philip Sidney and the Sonneteers

Sidney was born in 1554 and died of wounds sustained in the Netherlands campaign in 1586. During his short life he was courtier, traveler, diplomat, statesman, and soldier. His writings, mostly left unfinished, were the recreations of a life devoted to practical tasks. He was working on an expanded version of his *Arcadia* just before he set out on his last expedition; his translation of the Psalms was completed by his sister, the Countess of Pembroke; and his translation of Mornay's treatise on the truth of the Christian religion was completed by Arthur Golding, who is better known for his version of

Ovid's *Metamorphoses*. But in spite of his early death and the distractions of public affairs, Sidney excelled in three different fields: criticism, prose romance, and poetry.

The immediate occasion for *The Defense of Poesy*—in another edition of the same year (1595) it was entitled *An Apology for Poetry*—was the publication, with a dedication to Sidney, of Stephen Gosson's *School of Abuse,* a violent attack on poets and playwrights for their bad effect on the country's morals. Gosson, who was himself an unsuccessful and repentant poet and dramatist, knew that Sidney was a serious-minded Protestant, but was probably unaware that he had written a masque, that he had begun *Arcadia,* and that he was a friend of Edmund Spenser. The dedication, therefore, was singularly inept. According to Spenser, Gosson "was for his labour scorned: if at least it be in the goodness of that nature to scorn." In *The Defence of Poesy,* Sidney does not refer to Gosson, though he replies incidentally to some of his arguments. (The most recent editor of *The Defence,* Geoffrey Shepherd, denies that it was written as a reply to Gosson.) The purpose of *The Defence* was twofold: to answer general attacks on poetry —that it had a bad effect on manners and morals, that it was untrue, and that Plato had wisely banished poets from his ideal Republic—and to survey the state of poetry in 1580. Sidney was writing before the work of the University Wits had transformed the outlook for the theater; and the only English play he could praise was *Gorboduc,* despite its regrettable violation of the unity of time. Nondramatic poetry, he knew, had declined in quality since Chaucer's *Troilus and Criseyde*; but he could hail Spenser's *The Shepherd's Calendar,* published in the previous year, as the first fruits of the poetic renaissance he confidently expected to see.

Sidney could condemn all the drama and most of the poetry of his own age without weakening his defense. He showed that poets could not be dismissed as liars because they did not pretend that what they wrote was literally true. Plato banished poets from the Republic because they propagated false ideas about the gods; and here Sidney appears to evade Plato's objections. He goes on to argue that the obscenity of some poetry does not prove that "poetry abuseth man's wit, but that man's wit abuseth poetry." Since poetry is more philosophical than history—not circumscribed by the necessity of recording facts—it cannot be regarded as a frivolous pursuit. Good poetry has a didactic purpose, the more effective because it gives pleasure while it instructs. Delightful teaching is, in fact, "the end of poesy." The poet, unlike other teachers,

> beginneth not with obscure definitions, which must blur the margent with interpretations, and load the memory with doubtfulness; but he cometh to you with words set in delightful proportion, either accompanied with, or prepared for, the well-enchanting skill of music; and with a tale forsooth he cometh unto you, with a tale which holdeth children from play, and old men from the chimney-corner. And, pretending no more, doth intend the winning of the mind from wickedness to virtue; even as the child is often brought to take most wholesome things by hiding them in such other as have a pleasant taste.

It is more effective to show an ambitious or angry man in a play than to preach against anger or ambition. Comedy represents people behaving so ridiculously that "it is impossible that any beholder can be content to be such a one"; tragedy makes "kings fear to be tyrants," reveals hidden sins, and teaches the uncertainty of this world; and epic poetry presents us with portraits of heroes —Achilles or Aeneas—in such a way that we wish to emulate them. The poet, unlike the philosopher, delights the learned and the unlearned alike.

Sidney had studied a number of previous critics, Aristotle, Horace, Scaliger, Castelvetro, and Minturno among others, and most of his arguments were not original; but he presented them in a new way and with different emphases. His style, which avoids technical jargon and rhetorical inflation, is the reflection of a singularly attractive personality: the style is the man. He uses a prose that is close to that of ordinary speech; but he can be eloquent and witty when occasion serves, and he uses many memorable phrases and apt illustrations. It is the first English critical essay, admirable in its poise and tone: it is addressed to an educated reader, not to a coterie. Compared with Shelley's *Defence of Poetry,* Sidney's may seem rather naïve in its arguments; but it is also without the prophetic tone that has irritated some of Shelley's modern readers.

Sidney's taste, which embraces "Chevy Chase" as well as Chaucer, was not at all narrow; but his criticisms of contemporary drama had a narrowing effect on his followers in the Countess of Pembroke's circle. They all turned their backs on the great drama written after Sidney's death, believing that he would have done the same. They tried to write the academic Senecan dramas he had seemed to advocate, supposing absurdly that plays ought not to be written for the stage. The Countess translated a French Senecan play about Antony; Daniel wrote a companion piece on Cleopatra; Samuel Brandon, one on Octavia; and Fulke Greville, three unactable Senecan tragedies. Even Thomas Kyd, who normally wrote for the professional stage, translated Garnier's *Cornelie*. The conditions of the Elizabethan theater prevented the greater dramatists from adopting Sidney's views on the unities and so producing classical plays to rival those of Corneille and Racine.

In one way *The Defence of Poesy* may be regarded as a manifesto of the group of poets associated with Sidney—Spenser, Dyer, and Greville—but the best way to counter Gosson's attack would have been to produce the kind of poetry that Sidney advocated, the sort that taught delightfully. Sidney's translation of the Psalms is certainly edifying, but it does not give much delight. In this field Sidney's attempts were surpassed by those of his sister. The attempts by Sidney and Spenser, egged on by Gabriel Harvey, to introduce classical meters into English poetry were an abortive experiment that produced only one or two poems that can be read for pleasure. But Sidney had begun *Arcadia* to amuse his sister; and this does succeed in teaching and delighting. He had pointed out in *The Defence*—as Shelley was later to do —that one can be a versifier without being a poet, and a poet without writing verse; and his contemporaries recognized *Arcadia* as poetry. "Sir Philip Sidney writ his immortal poem *Arcadia* in prose," said Francis Meres, "and yet our rarest poet."

Sidney's chief model was Sannazaro's *Arcadia,* which alternated prose narrative with poetic eclogues, and this plan was followed in Sidney's first version, eclogues being inserted after each book. But it seems certain, too, that Sidney's more complex story was suggested by Heliodorus' *Aethiopian History,* which had appeared some years before in Underdowne's translation. (See below, p. 112.)

The "old" *Arcadia* was soon circulating in manuscript, but Sidney became dissatisfied with it. He had failed to follow Horace's advice and classical precedent of beginning in the middle of the story, and the eclogues were charming irrelevancies. He therefore abandoned the chronological order of events and introduced a number of new episodes so that the general plan of the book resembled that of Ariosto's *Orlando Furioso*. It is therefore much more difficult to follow the story in the revised version, and Hazlitt called it "one of the greatest monuments of the abuse of the intellectual power on record." But Hazlitt lived before the complexities of the modern novel, and the "new" *Arcadia* can give considerable intellectual pleasure. Unfortunately, however, Sidney did not live to complete his task, and the first edition (1590) consisted of only three books. Three years later, the conclusion of the story was added by the Countess of Pembroke from the old *Arcadia,* but the mixture of old and new is confusing.

Arcadia has been described by Mona Wilson as "an encyclopedia of moral and political science." Sidney intended the behavior of some of his characters to serve as a model, and the behavior of others to serve as a warning, to his readers. We see virtuous people, such as Philoclea, one of the two heroines, resisting temptation; and we see evil characters, such as Cecropia, Philoclea's aunt, behaving hypocritically and cruelly. In the episode of the Paphlagonian King (which Shakespeare used for the underplot of *King Lear*) the ingratitude of one son is contrasted with the love and compassion shown by the other.

Fulke Greville, writing of *Arcadia,* declared of Sidney that

> In all these creatures of his making, his interest and scope was to turn the barren philosophy precepts into pregnant images of life; and in them, first on the monarch's part, lively to represent the growth, state and declination of princes, change of government and laws . . . Then, again, in the subject's case, the state of favour, disfavour, prosperity, adversity . . . and all other moods of private fortunes or misfortunes, in which traverses, I know, his purpose was to limn out such exact pictures of every posture in the mind, that any man might see how to set a good countenance upon all the discountenances of adversity.

Perhaps Greville, whose mind was more somber than Sidney's and who, by the time he wrote these words, was disillusioned, exaggerated the didactic element in *Arcadia,* which is primarily a romantic tale and only secondarily didactic. But although Sidney wrote the book for "recreation," he was able to instruct at the same time.

There are more than a hundred characters in the book, and most of them are merely types, exemplifying the virtues, vices, and other characteristics about which Sidney was writing. There is little or no psychological analysis in the book, and it is nearer to the epic than it is to the novel. But it was the first Elizabethan masterpiece, worthy to stand beside *The Faerie Queene*; it remained popular for a hundred years; it was the model for many later writers of prose and a quarry to which many dramatists went for plots; and it was a work of wit and worth (as Milton grudgingly admitted in writing of Charles I's fondness for it[1]).

Sidney writes prose with conscious artistry, while avoiding the excessive artificiality of Lyly's euphuism. Sometimes he uses conceits that to a modern reader ar faintly absurd, as when the princesses, undressing bath, are described as "getting the pure silve bodies out of the ore of their garments de- scribed Sidney's prose as "the embr nnest art and daintiest wit"; but it is at its b t in the em- broidery, but in the subtle cadences of his descriptive passages, as when he concludes a long and complex sentence about the country of Arcadia with the words:

> each pasture stored with sheep feeding with sober security, while the pretty lambs with bleating oratory craved the dams' comfort; here a shepherd's boy piping, as though he should never be old; there a young shepherdess knit- ting, and withal singing, and it seemed that her voice comforted her hands to work, and her hands kept time to her voice's music.

Sidney is also splendid in some of his long, argumentative speeches. When Cecropia, for example, is trying to per- suade Philoclea to marry, she uses very persuasive argu- ments, as the devil can cite Scripture. When Shakespeare was writing his early sonnets, urging Mr. W. H. to marry, he was able, without any incongruity, to use some of Cecropia's images:

> Have you ever seen a pure rosewater kept in a crystal glass? How fine it looks, how sweet it smells, while that beautiful glass imprisons it! Break the prison, and let the water take his own course, doth it not embrace dust, and

[1] *Eikonoklastes,* Chapter I.

lose all his former sweetness and fairness? Truly, so are we, if we have not the stay, rather than the restraint, of crystalline marriage.

It is not surprising that one Elizabethan writer on rhetoric, Abraham France, was able to illustrate all the figures of rhetoric from *Arcadia*.

The third of Sidney's important works, the sonnet sequence *Astrophel and Stella,* was probably written in 1582, soon after the marriage of Penelope Devereux to Lord Rich and before Sidney's own marriage to Frances Walsingham in 1583. Although Sir Sidney Lee declared that "detachment from the realities of ordinary passion . . . is the central feature of Sidney's sonnets" [2] and that he derived his inspiration not from his love for Penelope Devereux, but from Italian sonneteers, nearly all critics believe that the sequence reflects the poet's genuine feelings. This does not mean, of course, that there are not elements of dramatization and even of invention. The sonnet describing Stella on the Thames may well be based on Petrarch's description of Laura on the river Po rather than on an actual incident. But there are no sonnets in Sidney's sequence that are translated from foreign originals; and the fact that Sidney was writing in a convention does not mean that he was not also writing from experience. Modes of love have often been influenced by literature.

The first edition of *Astrophel and Stella,* published piratically in 1591, five years after Sidney's death and three years after Penelope Rich had left her husband, has an atrociously bad text; but it contains a modish preface by Thomas Nashe that describes the book as

[2] *Elizabethan Sonnets* (London: Constable, 1904).

"the tragi-comedy of love . . . performed by starlight
. . . the argument, cruel chastity; the prologue, hope;
the epilogue, despair." The sequence describes how
Astrophel falls in love with Stella when it is too late—a
proposed betrothal of Sidney and Penelope had fallen
through—and how she resists his attempts to seduce
her. Two sonnets that are often printed at the end of the
sequence—"Thou blind man's mark, thou fool's self-
chosen snare" and "Leave me, O Love, which reachest
but to dust"—although they round off the story neatly
are probably not related to it, and may well have been
written earlier.

Charles Lamb pointed out that, unlike most sonnet
sequences, Sidney's is not vague and unlocalized. The
sonnets are

> full, material and circumstantiated. Time and place ap-
> propriates every one of them. It is not a fever of passion
> wasting itself upon a thin diet of dainty words, but a
> transcendent passion pervading and illuminating action,
> pursuits, studies, feats of arms, the opinions of contem-
> poraries, and his judgment of them. An historical thread
> runs through them, which almost affixes a date to them;
> marks the when and where they were written.[3]

Astrophel and Stella tells a more coherent story than
any other sequence and, apart only from Shakespeare's,
a more dramatic one. Both the protagonists are rent by
inner conflict: Stella is prevented by honor from capitu-
lating—Penelope, unlike Stella, was in love with another man—and Astrophel, striving to consummate his
love, is less aware of its sinfulness than of the way it

---

[3] "Some Sonnets of Sir Philip Sydney" (*sic*) in *Last Essays of
Elia*.

distracts him from his duties. In several of the sonnets
he bitterly reproaches himself for wasting his talents:

> What what sharp checks I in myself am shent,
> When into Reason's audit I do go:
> And by just counts myself a bankrupt know
> Of all those goods which heaven to me hath lent,
> Unable quite to pay even Nature's rent
> Which unto it by birthright I do owe.

In another sonnet he acknowledges the justice of a
friend's criticisms—his young mind marred, his wits
lame in virtue, his lack of achievement—and then
replies:

> Sure you say well: your wisdom's golden mine
> Dig deep with Learning's spade. Now tell me this:
> Hath this world ought so fair as Stella is?

His friends, seeing him "oft in dark abstracted guise,"
imagine that he is thinking of state affairs, but he is
thinking only of Stella. At first he is overjoyed when
Stella confesses that she loves him, but this platonic affection soon ceases to satisfy. "Desire still cries: 'Give
me some food.'" Although he says that "Venus is
taught with Dian's wings to fly," he still hopes to go
beyond the kiss that Stella has permitted. The climax
of the action is told, not in sonnets, but in two of the
interspersed songs. In one (No. 4) Astrophel presses his
suit in Stella's room, and she declines to surrender to
his pleading. The poem is an exquisite expression of the
central situation of the sequence:

> Only joy! now here you are
> Fit to hear and ease my care,
> Let my whispering voice obtain
> Sweet rewards for sharpest pain;

Take me to thee, and thee to me.
No, no, no, no, my Dear, let be.

Night hath closed all in her cloak,
Twinkling stars love-thoughts provoke,
Danger hence good care doth keep,
Jealousy himself doth sleep;
Take me to thee, and thee to me.
No, no, no, no, my Dear, let be.

Better place no wit can find,
Cupid's knot to loose or bind;
Those sweet flowers on fine bed too,
Us in their best language woo.
Take me to thee, and thee to me.
No, no, no, no, my Dear, let be.

. . .

Niggard Time threats, if we miss
This large offer of our bliss,
Long stay, ere he grant the same:
Sweet, then, while each thing doth frame,
Take me to thee, and thee to me.
No, no, no, no, my Dear, let be.

Your fair mother is a-bed,
Candles out and curtains spread.
She thinks you do letters write:
Write, but first let me indite:
"Take me to thee, and thee to me."
No, no, no, no, my Dear, let be.

Sweet, alas, why strive you thus?
Concord better fitteth us.
Leave to Mars the force of hands,
Your power in your beauty stands.
Take me to thee, and thee to me.
No, no, no, no, my Dear, let be.

Woe to me! and do you swear
Me to hate, but I forbear?

> Cursed be my destines all
> That brought me so high to fall!
> Soon with my death I will please thee.
> *No, no, no, no, my Dear, let be.*

Later, this time in a grove, she replies to his pleadings:

> Tyrant Honour doth thus use thee:
> Stella's self might not refuse thee.

The remainder of the sequence is concerned with Astrophel's despair.

In *The Defence of Poesy* Sidney had remarked that

> If I were a mistress, sonneteers would never persuade me they were in love; so coldly they apply fiery speeches as men that had rather read lovers' writings, and so caught up certain swelling phrases . . . than that in truth they feel those passions.

When, therefore, Sidney wrote his own sonnets, he was determined to avoid this fault. In the very first sonnet he rejects the studying of fine inventions and the imitation of previous sonneteers; he is at the command of his Muse to look into his heart and write. In the third sonnet he rejects those who flaunt themselves in fine phrases; and in later sonnets he contrasts his own sincerity with the exaggeration of other poets. This avowal of sincerity is itself a convention of Italian and French sonneteers; but nevertheless, Sidney adopted a colloquial style in many of the sonnets so that they give the impression of what Keats called "the true voice of feeling."

A number of the early sonnets, however, are conventional in style: they may have been written when Sidney was attracted by Stella's beauty, but was not yet deeply in love. Their weaknesses may be due to the fact that he did not at once find his own style, or, as I have suggested elsewhere, he may have wished to show how

Astrophel—who should not be completely identified with the poet—progressed from a conventional love to a genuine passion. Shakespeare similarly distinguished Romeo's speeches about Rosaline with his speeches to Juliet.

Even the later sonnets vary a good deal in quality. There are awkwardnesses of expression, unhappy conceits, and clumsy inversions for the sake of a rhyme, faults that Sidney might have eliminated if he had ever contemplated publication. But, when all is said, no other sonnet sequence gives such an impression of truth, Shakespeare's only excepted; there are few Elizabethan sonnets as fine as Sidney's best; and some of the interspersed songs are, as we have seen, even better than the sonnets. Among the greatest sonnets are "With how sad steps, O Moon, thou climb'st the skies" and the one addressed to sleep:

> Come sleep, O sleep, the certain knot of peace,
> The baiting place of wit, the balm of woe,
> The poor man's wealth, the prisoner's release,
> Th' indifferent judge between the high and low,
> With shield of proof shield me from out the prease
> Of those fierce darts Despair at me doth throw;
> O make in me those civil wars to cease!
> I will good tribute pay if thou do so.
> Take thou of me smooth pillows, sweetest bed,
> A chamber deaf to noise and blind to light,
> A rosy garland, and a weary head,
> And if these things, as being thine by right,
> > Move not thy heavy grace, thou shalt in me,
> > Livelier than elsewhere, Stella's image see.

Most of Sidney's other verse is of minor importance; but while he was writing *Arcadia,* he experimented in many different forms. Harvey rightly said that there was none "like him for gallant variety." *Arcadia* could be

used as a textbook on different verse forms. There are
poems in terza rima, madrigals, sonnets, double sestinas,
an epithalamium, and many other forms. The sonnets
include the famous one beginning, "My true love hath
my heart, and I have his." Scattered through these poems
are lines as exquisite as any in *Astrophel and Stella*:

> Delay, the rack of unrefrained desire . . .
> These stately stars in their new-shining faces,

but the *Arcadia* poems are mainly interesting as the
means by which Sidney acquired his technique.

Two of his masterpieces, however, are not in the sonnet sequence. One is the beautiful nightingale poem,
"The nightingale, as soon as April bringeth," in which
Sidney obtains a charming musical effect by using only
feminine rhymes. The other is the spirited litany on the
death of love, which begins:

> Ring out your bells, let mourning shows be spread,
>   For love is dead:
> All love is dead, infected
>   With plague of deep disdain;
> Worth, as nought worth, rejected,
>   And Faith fair scorn doth gain.
>   From so ungrateful fancy,
>   From such a female frenzy,
>   From them that use men thus,
>   Good Lord, deliver us.

There is no reason to believe that this poem was written
on the occasion of Penelope Devereux's marriage with
Lord Rich since Sidney was not then in love with her.

FULKE GREVILLE, LORD BROOKE

At about the same time as Sidney was writing *Astrophel and Stella,* his friend Fulke Greville (1554–1628)

began a rival sequence, *Caelica,* which was not published until nearly half a century later. Some of Greville's poems were written with Sidney's in mind. No. 75, for example, like Sidney's eighth song, consists of a dialogue between lovers in the spring. The two poets are refused by their mistresses; but whereas Stella refuses Astrophel because of tyrant Honor, Caelica refuses Philocell because, as she says:

> My delight is all my care,
> All laws else despised are.
> I will never rumour move,
> At least for one I do not love.

But the resemblances between the two sequences serve only to throw into relief the differences between the two poets. Sidney writes only of Stella; Greville names Myra, Caelica, and Cynthia in his poems, though they were not necessarily three different women. Sidney is the devoted Petrarchan lover; Greville varies his devotion with cynicism and contempt and a doubt whether women can be constant:

> And who entreats, you know entreats in vain,
> That love be constant, or come back again.

It is lines like these that have led critics to suggest that Greville's attitude to love is as realistic as Donne's.

Little more than a third of the *Caelica* poems are in sonnet form; and, in the last twenty-five, Greville says farewell to Cupid and devotes himself to philosophical and religious themes. The general impression one gets of *Caelica* as a whole is that it is an antilove sequence. Greville is ironical, somber, and pessimistic. He said in later years that his poetry was addressed to the disillusioned:

not to them on whose foot the black ox had not trod,
as the proverb is, but to those only that are weather-
beaten in the sea of this world, such as having lost the
sight of their gardens and groves, study to sail on a right
course among rocks and quicksands.

He seems more at home with the religious and didactic
subjects he deals with in the latter part of the sequence
than he is with love. Yet the two most satisfactory poems
are concerned with love. One is a delightful song, later
set to music, which has a gaiety and spirit Greville does
not elsewhere display:

> Away with these self-loving lads,
> Whom Cupid's arrow never glads!
> Away, poor souls, that sigh and weep,
> In love of those that lie asleep!
>   For Cupid is a meadow-god,
>   And forceth none to kiss the rod.

The other poem complains of female inconstancy, but in
a good-humored way. The first four stanzas are beautifully turned; the last one begins with a charming conceit, but it ends with three rather disjointed aphorisms:

> I, with whose colours Myra dressed her head,
> I, that ware posies of her own hand-making;
> I, that mine own name in the chimneys read
> By Myra finely wrought ere I was waking:
>   Must I look on, in hope time coming may
>   With change bring back my turn again to play?
>
> I, that on Sunday at the church-stile found
> A garland sweet, with true-love knots in flowers,
> Which I to wear about mine arm was bound,
> That each of us might know that all was ours:
>   Must I now lead an idle life in wishes?
>   And follow Cupid for his loaves and fishes?
>
> I, that did wear the ring her mother left,
> I, for whose love she gloried to be blamed;

I, with whose eyes her eyes committed theft,
I, who did make her blush when I was named:
    Must I lose ring, flowers, blush, theft and go naked,
    Watching with sighs till dead love be awaked?

I, that when drowsy Argus fell asleep,
Like Jealousy o'erwatched with desire,
Was ever warned modesty to keep,
While her breath, speaking, kindled Nature's fire:
    Must I look on a-cold, while others warm them?
    Do Vulcan's brothers in such fine nets arm them?

Was it for this that I might Myra see
Washing the water with her beauties, white?
Yet would she never write her love to me;
Thinks wit of change while thoughts are in delight?
    Mad girls must safely love, as they may leave;
    No man can print a kiss, lines may deceive.

In the farewell to Cupid, the last of the love poems,
Greville declares that he will play

With thoughts that please me less, and less betray me.

In the remainder of the sequence, dealing with thoughts
that pleased him less, he seems to have intended to write
on the heavenly love that "is the peace whereto all
thoughts do strive"; but his religious views were too
somber, his belief in the corruption of man's heart too
deeply rooted, for him to find much peace. He exhorts
man to endure his self, to "dream no more of curious
mysteries," to recognize that human glory is hollow,
that eternal truth is "exiled from man's fleshly heart,"
and that we cannot miraculously cure our habits. The
living Lord is "a God unknown," and our one hope of
redemption is a firm conviction of our wickedness.

This profound pessimism formed the basis of Greville's
later work. It included a prose work, misleadingly en-

titled *The Life of Sir Philip Sidney* (1652)—which is mainly an apologia for his own writings—and a series of verse treatises. These latter are filled with shrewd remarks, often in the form of aphorisms, but they gain very little from being written in verse. Greville came to regard poetry as a mere instrument for the expression of thought, and he distrusted rhetoric. He deliberately used prosaic diction, and even his imagery is used prosaically. His most effective lines are the result of compression rather than of beautiful phrasing, as in the line about war:

> Where the unhappy only happy are.

He had, at least in his later work, a prose mind; and he tried in his verse to maintain the virtues of prose. He retained rhyme, but he distrusted metaphor, hyperbole, and most other poetical devices. He condemns rhetoric because it "stains the matron with the harlot's weed." Beauty ought to be strictly functional since the best words are those "Which do most properly express the thought." Eloquence is not a craft of words but "Such as from living wisdoms do proceed." Poetry is "Only as pleasing sauce to dainty food"; and its true function is to describe goodness or God and to help us to control our passions. Greville's best editor, Professor Geoffrey Bullough, suggests that if he had written his treatises in prose he would have been a great moral and political essayist, although, it should be added, a reactionary and pessimistic one.

The largest section of Greville's work consists of treatises in verse on human learning, on fame and honor, on monarchy, and on religion. Together they provide a gloomy commentary on man's pretensions. Human learning, he believed, was corrupted by original sin and was therefore worthless. The elect do not need learning, but, on the other hand, ignorance is the mother of every lust. He agreed with Bacon that science should be based on experiment. Men must be terrorized into obedience and conformity by the laws. The desire for glory is a sin, but it may be a necessary spur to make men avoid shame. The world's religion is born of wit and lust; but true religion can restore God's image in man. The visible church is corrupt; the invisible church consists of the followers of Christ, who are necessarily few in number:

> They do in praying, and still pray in doing;
> Faith and obedience are their contemplation;
> Like lovers still admiring, ever wooing
> Their God, that gives this heavenly constellation.

They seem fools to the world; they despise the arts, book learning, and even theology; and they serve as a reproach to the priests of the visible church. Greville was anti-humanist and antipoetic in his views; but in his old age he looked back nostalgically to the age of Elizabeth and the age of Sidney before the black ox had trodden on his feet.

His plays are much more interesting. They were not intended for the stage. "It was no part of my purpose," he said, "to write for them against whom so many and great spirits have already written." His models were the French Senecan plays, which were so much admired in the Sidney circle, but he differs from his models in his use of the choruses for even lengthier discourses on political and religious topics. He disapproved of the Greek dramatists who exemplify "the disastrous miseries of man's life" and so make us murmur against divine providence; and he did not attempt, as he imagined his contemporaries did, "to point out God's revenging aspect upon every particular sin." His plays were political. They attempted "to trace out the high ways of ambitious governors" and the desolation and ruin they bring upon themselves.[4]

Greville wrote three tragedies but destroyed one on the subject of Antony and Cleopatra because he was afraid that it would be taken to refer to the fate of Essex. *Philotas,* by his friend Daniel, had gotten its author into trouble for the same reason. The two tragedies that survive, *Mustapha* (1609) and *Alaham,* were probably written before the end of the sixteenth century and revised afterward. They are based on contemporary history, and they both show the evils of tyranny, with the moral that although rebellion against evil kings is never justifiable, misgovernment by tyrants would drive their subjects to rebel. Greville had little dramatic power and a complete inability to vary his style to suit the different characters. His style is not obscure; but the rhythm of his lines is curiously wooden and disjointed, the lines are end-stopped, and the irregularity of the rhyming teases the ear. Greville had no skill in construction; the tragic events are merely occasions for moralizing comments; and the characters are puppets. In the last few minutes of *Alaham,* there are two murders, a suicide, and the death of the protagonist, but the events fail to excite because of the undramatic dialogue:

> Flesh is too weak, it hath satiety.
> Lust, intermittent here; and Fury, poor;

[4] *Life of Sir Philip Sidney,* ed. N. Smith (Oxford: Clarendon Press, 1907), pp. 221ff.

Rage hath respects, desires here weary be.
Leave Man this mean: let us live in excess,
Where power is more, although the joys be less.

In spite of these weaknesses, which make *Mustapha* and *Alaham* abortive as dramas, the two plays contain some of Greville's finest poetry. The political argument is more poetical than it is in the treatises, and the choruses are particularly fine. The third chorus of *Mustapha,* a dialogue between Time and Eternity, has touches of splendor; and the two antithetical choruses at the end of the play are the high-water mark of Greville's poetry. In the first of these the Tartars attack supernatural religion as vain superstition, "child of false miracles." They satirize those who regard the afterlife as all-important, believing that nothing is the

way unto eternal being,
Death to salvation, and the grave to heaven.

They urge man to trust to Nature:

Her mysteries are read without Faith's eyesight:
She speaketh in our flesh; and from our senses
Delivers down her wisdoms to our reason.

To this the second chorus, of priests, argues that it is useless to rely on nature and that it is equally vain to seek salvation in ritual or dogma, since the priest who looks into his own heart finds a god there, "far unlike his books." Although these priests are not, of course, Christian, the ideas they express fit in with Greville's insistence, in the treatise on religion, that man should have an individual relationship with God:

O wearisome condition of Humanity!
Born under one law, to another bound!

Vainly begot, and yet forbidden vanity,
Created sick, commanded to be sound.
  What meaneth Nature by these diverse laws?
  Passion and Reason self-division cause.

Is it the mark or majesty of Power
To make offences that it may forgive?
Nature herself doth her own self deflower,
To hate those errors she herself doth give.
  For how should man think that he may not do,
  If Nature did not fail, and punish too?

Tyrant to others, to herself unjust,
Only commands things difficult and hard;
Forbids us all things which it knows is lust,
Makes easy pains, unpossible reward:
  If Nature did not take delight in blood,
  She would have made more easy ways to good.

We that are bound by vows and by promotion,
With pomp of holy sacrifice and rites,
To teach belief in good and still devotion,
To preach of heaven's wonders and delights:
  Yet when each of us in his own heart looks
  He finds the God there, far unlike his books.

The apparently skeptical modernity of this passage
led Aldous Huxley to use the first stanza as the epigraph
to *Point Counter Point* and made another critic speak of
Greville as the greatest of Elizabethan poets after Shakespeare. The verdict is a strange one, for although Greville
had an interesting mind, he was not, except at rare moments, a good, and only on one occasion was he a great,
poet; and those who are attracted by his skepticism
should remember what he said of himself—that he
knew the world and believed in God.

THE VOGUE OF THE SONNET

Hardly any sonnets were published between 1557 and 1591, but *Astrophel and Stella* was such a success that poets who had not attempted to imitate the sonnets of Wyatt and Surrey in Tottel's *Songs and Sonnets* now hastened to imitate Sidney's sequence. In 1592 appeared Samuel Daniel's *Delia* and Henry Constable's *Diana*; in the following year, Barnabe Barnes' *Parthenophil and Parthenope,* Thomas Lodge's *Phillis,* Giles Fletcher's *Licia,* and Thomas Watson's *The Tears of Fancy.* (Watson's earlier *Hecatompathia* had been a collection of sixteen-line poems.) William Percy's *Coelia,* Michael Drayton's *Idea's Mirror,* and the anonymous *Zepheria* followed in 1594; Richard Barnfield's *Cynthia* and Spenser's *Amoretti* in 1595; Bartholomew Griffin's *Fidessa,* Richard Linche's *Diella,* and William Smith's *Chloris* in 1596; and Robert Tofte's *Laura* in 1597. Shakespeare's and Greville's sonnets were probably written during the same period, but were not published until the seventeenth century; and there were later sequences by William Habington (1634) and by two Scottish poets, Sir William Alexander (1604) and William Drummond of Hawthornden (1616). In addition to these love sonnets, there were a number of religious and philosophical sequences by George Chapman, Constable, Barnes, and others, culminating in the Divine Sonnets of John Donne.

Several of these sonneteers are discussed in other chapters, but it will be appropriate to discuss here the extent of Sidney's influence. Some of Spenser's sonnets may have been written before *Astrophel and Stella,* but it may have been Sidney's example that led him to arrange them

so as to tell, if somewhat vaguely, his courtship of Elizabeth Boyle. Shakespeare's sonnets, badly arranged as they
appear to be, convey a coherent story. None of the remaining love sequences has any narrative interest. The
poets produced only collections of individual sonnets, or
groups of sonnets, linked, if at all, by the fact that they
are addressed to one woman, real or imaginary, a Delia,
an Idea, or an Aurora. The impetus to write sonnets
came largely from the success of *Astrophel and Stella*;
but many of the poets imitated French and Italian sequences, and some went further afield. Giles Fletcher's
Licia (1593), to take an extreme case, contains at least
forty translations from Angerianus, Marullus, Muretus,
and Gruterus. More than a score of the sonnets in
Lodge's *Phillis* (1593) have been traced to Ariosto,
Paschale, Ronsard, Desportes, and others; several of
Drayton's sonnets are derived from Scève; and about a
third of Daniel's were suggested by French and Italian
poems. These facts are mentioned not to impugn the
sincerity of the Elizabethan sonneteers, but merely to
show that they wrote in a European tradition, which the
success of *Astrophel and Stella* fanned into a flame in
England.

The minor poets wished to emulate Sidney rather than
to express their own emotions; but, since life sometimes
imitates art, they may have used the ideas of earlier poets
to express their love. It would be impossible on internal
evidence to decide which of their sonnets were original
and which were imitations—they have failures and
successes of both kinds. Fletcher admitted on his title
page that he was writing imitations of "the best Latin
Poets, and others"; but although the other poets did not

generally acknowledge their indebtedness, there is no reason to accuse them of dishonesty. They were taught at school to imitate Latin writers; and all poets, good and bad, incorporated in their work echoes of earlier authors, echoes that their readers would appreciate as readers of T. S. Eliot's poems enjoy spotting echoes from Dante, Baudelaire, Middleton, Andrewes, and St. John of the Cross.

The first twelve lines of the following sonnet by Thomas Lodge are closely based on one by Ariosto; but he deviates from the original in the final couplet and thereby spoils what would otherwise be a good poem:

> Not causeless were you christened, gentle flowers,
> The one of faith, the other fancy's pride;
> For she who guides both faith and fancy's power
> In your fair colours wraps her ivory side.
> As one of you hath whiteness without stain,
> So spotless is my love and never tainted;
> And as the other shadoweth faith again,
> Such is my lass, with no fond change acquainted,
> And as nor tyrant sun nor winter weather
> May ever change sweet amaranthus' hue,
> So she, though love and fortune join together,
> Will never leave to be both fair and true.
>   And should I leave thee there, thou pretty elf?
>   Nay, first let Damon quite forget himself.

Many of the sonneteers were mere poetasters, trying to be in the swim; and one or two were atrociously bad. Tofte does not have a single tolerable sonnet in his collection; and the anonymous author of *Zepheria* (1594) had a positive genius for inflated diction and absurd imagery. Below are four examples from that work:

> When I emprized, though in my love's affections,
> The silver lustre of thy brow to unmask,

Though hath my Muse hyperbolised trajections;
Yet stands it aye deficient to such task.

. . .

Beauty! peculiar parent of Conceit!
Prosperous midwife to a travelling Muse!

. . .

My heart prepares anew to thesaurize
Sighs and love options such as it sent of yore.

. . .

'Mongst Delian nymphs, in Angels' university,
Thou, my Zepheria, liv'st matriculated!

One would like to think that the author of these lines
was being intentionally funny. If so, his intentions were
misunderstood even by his contemporaries, for he was
one of the poets parodied by Sir John Davies in his
"gulling" sonnets:

The lover under burthen of his mistress' love,
Which like to Ætna did his heart oppress,
Did give such piteous groans that he did move
The heavens at length to pity his distress.
But, for the fates in their high court above
Forbade to make the grievous burden less,
The gracious powers did all conspire to prove
If miracle this mischief might redress.
Therefore regarding that the load was such
As no man might with one man's might sustain,
And that mild patience imported much
To him that should endure an endless pain,
 By their decree he soon transformed was
 Into a patient burden-bearing ass.

But, despite the feebleness of many sonnets of the
period, it should be recognized that even very minor
poets had occasional successes. Bartholemew Griffin (d.
1602), for example, who is mostly a flat, dull, and incompetent versifier, contrived to write one sonnet that is
not without charm:

Fair is my love that feeds among the lilies,
The lilies growing in that pleasant garden
Where Cupid's Mount, that well-beloved hill is,
And where that little god himself is warden.
See where my love sits in the beds of spices!
Beset all round with camphor, myrrh, and roses;
And interlaced with curious devices
Which her from all the world apart encloses.
There doth she tune her lute for her delight,
And with sweet music makes the ground to move;
Whilst I, poor I, do sit in heavy plight,
Wailing alone my unrespected love.
    Not daring rush into so rare a place,
    That gives to her, and she to it, a grace.

There are, moreover, a number of well-turned sonnets
in the later miscellanies—*The Phoenix Nest* and *The
Poetical Rhapsody*—and Barnes and Constable, whose
love sonnets are imitative and entirely undistinguished,
produced much better poetry when they turned to religious themes; and the same thing may be said of Drummond. This can be illustrated by a comparison of one of
Constable's best secular sonnets with one of his religious
ones:

My lady's presence makes the roses red,
Because to see her lips they blush for shame
The lily's leaves for envy pale became
And her white hands in them this envy bred.
The marigold abroad her leaves did spread
Because the sun's and her power is the same.
The violet of purple colour came,
Dyed with the blood she made my heart to shed
In brief, all flowers from her their virtue take,
From her sweet breath their sweet smells do proceed;
The living heat, which her eyebeams do make
Warmeth the ground and quickeneth the seed.
    The rain, wherewith she watereth these flowers,
    Falls from mine eyes which she dissolves in showers.

In that, O Queen of queens, thy birth was free
From guilt, which others do of grace bereave,
When in their mother's womb they life receive,
God, as his sole-born daughter, loved thee.
To match thee like thy birth's nobility,
He thee His spirit for thy spouse did leave,
Of whom thou did'st His only son conceive,
And so was linked to all the Trinity.
Cease then, O queens! who earthly crowns do wear,
To glory in the pomp of worldly things:
If men such high respect unto you bear,
Which daughters, wives and mothers are of kings,
 What honour should unto that Queen be done,
 Who had your God for father, spouse and son?

The love sonnet is one of Constable's best; but, even here, the conceits are both unoriginal and far-fetched. The religious sonnet, one of a group that was not published until long after the poet's death, is beautifully constructed and phrased; there is some pressure of thought behind it; and the last line is not merely a conceit, but also an epigrammatic expression of a deeply felt religious conviction.

Suggested Reading

The best edition of Sidney's poems is that of W. A. Ringler (Oxford: Clarendon Press, 1962). The collected works have been edited by A. Feuillerat (Cambridge Univ. Press, 1912–26). The best edition of *An Apology for Poetry (The Defence of Poesy)* is that of G. Shepherd (Edinburgh: Nelson, 1965). Among books on Sidney may be mentioned *Sir Philip Sidney* by Mona Wilson (London: Duckworth, 1931) and *Sir Philip Sidney as a Literary Craftsman* by K. O. Myrick (Cambridge, Mass.: Harvard Univ. Press, 1935). *Sir Philip Sidney* by Kenneth Muir (London: Longmans, 1960) is a brief introduction. Greville's *Poems and Dramas* have been edited by Geoffrey Bullough (Edinburgh: Oliver and Boyd, 1939); his *Remains* by G. A. Wilkes (Oxford Univ. Press, 1965); and his *Life of Sir Philip Sidney* by N. Smith (Oxford: Clarendon Press, 1907).

Many of the sonnet sequences were collected by Sidney Lee in *Elizabethan Sonnets* (London: Constable, 1904). There is a study, *Les Sonnets élisabéthains* by J. G. Scott (Paris: Champion, 1929). Constable's poems have been edited by Joan Grundy (Liverpool Univ. Press, 1960) and Habington's by Kenneth Allott (Liverpool Univ. Press, 1948).

IV
Two Professional Poets

SAMUEL DANIEL

Samuel Daniel (1563–1619) has suffered from Jonson's
scornful description of his verse:

> It runs and slides, and only makes a sound.
> Women's poets they are called, as you have women's
> tailors.
> They write a verse, as smooth, as soft, as cream;
> In which there is no torrent, nor scarce stream.

There is some truth in this. Daniel's work, even when
he deals with martial topics, is lacking in vigor and
masculinity; his love sonnets are quite without passion;
his plays were outside the main stream of Elizabethan

drama; and his masques were a failure. He was a careful and elegant craftsman whose inspiration was chiefly literary. Yet the admiration for his work, shared by Wordsworth and Coleridge and expressed in our own day by Bonamy Dobrée,[1] should warn us against dismissing Daniel as a minor poet of little interest.

His first appearance as a poet was in 1591, when twenty-seven of his sonnets were included in the surreptitious edition of *Astrophel and Stella*; and in the following year he republished his own sonnets under the title *Delia*. He was employed by the Countess of Pembroke as her son's tutor and encouraged by her to write. It was natural that he should take Sidney as his first model; that when he tried his hand at drama in *Cleopatra* (1594), he should write a sequel to the Countess' *Antonie,* translated from Garnier; and that he should adopt the style of the French Senecan school.

The *Delia* sequence may have been written about an actual woman—there seems otherwise no point in his changing in a later edition the color of Delia's hair from "golden" to "sable"—but his real theme was not so much love as time's threat to beauty:

> Men do not weigh the stalk for that it was,
> When once they find her flower, her glory pass.

These particular lines are from a pair of sonnets imitated from Tasso; and some twenty of Daniel's sonnets have been traced to foreign originals. But they are not direct translations: they are variations on a theme by another poet. Elizabethans were taught at school the art

---

[1] Bonamy Dobrée, *Restoration Tragedy, 1660–1720* (Oxford Univ. Press, 1929), appendix.

of writing by imitation of classical authors; and the earliest English sonnets were adapted by Wyatt from Petrarch. Sir Sidney Lee, who devoted years to proving that Elizabethan sonnets were insincere, declared that Daniel's best-known sonnet was a mere adaptation of Desportes; and there is little doubt that the opening lines are imitated directly from one of his sonnets:

> Care-charmer Sleep, son of the sable Night,
> Brother to Death, in silent darkness born.

But in the remaining twelve lines Daniel owes little or nothing to his source. This is typical of his method.

Nearly all of Daniel's sonnets are written in the Shakespearian form, three quatrains followed by a couplet, and the best of them are smoothly turned and musical, though they lack subtlety of thought and originality of imagery. Here is a typical one on the transience of beauty:

> Look, Delia, how we esteem the half-blown rose,
> The image of thy blush and summer's honour,
> Whilst yet her tender bud doth undisclose
> That full of beauty Time bestows upon her;
> No sooner spreads her glory in the air,
> But straight her wide-blown pomp comes to decline;
> She then is scorned, that late adorned the fair:
> So fade the roses of those cheeks of thine.
> No April can revive thy withered flowers
> Whose springing grace adorns thy glory now:
> Swift speedy Time, feathered with flying hours,
> Dissolves the beauty of the fairest brow.
> > Then do not thou such treasure waste in vain,
> > But love now whilst thou may'st be loved again.

The Complaint of Rosamond, published with *Delia,* is the best example of a genre that is often tedious and depressing. It was probably Daniel's use of rhyme royal and the suitability of this stanza for tragic laments that led Shakespeare to choose it for his *Lucrece*.

Cleopatra (1594), Daniel's next work was not intended for the stage, and it is about as undramatic as it could be. Years later, about the time of Shakespeare's play on the same subject, Daniel rewrote his, with the death of the heroine taking place on stage instead of being reported by messenger; but in the collected edition of his works (1623) the earlier version of the play was printed. Its action takes place after the death of Antony. Daniel makes little dramatic use of the conflict between Cleopatra and Octavius and his plan to take her to Rome in his triumph, which she foils by her suicide. Each act is followed by a moralizing chorus, and the dialogue is written mainly in rhymed quatrains. All the characters are static and statuesque; and Cleopatra herself has none of the variety and fascination, nor even the sensuality, that the story demands. This is partly because we see her only after the death of her lover. Daniel had taken to heart Sidney's criticisms of contemporary drama and done his best to write the kind of play of which the Countess of Pembroke would approve. In his dedication to her, Daniel speaks of the English Senecans:

> Now when so many pens (like spears) are charged
> To chase away this tyrant of the North,
> Gross Barbarism, whose power grown far enlarged
> Was lately by thy valiant brother's worth
> First found, encountered, and provoked forth;
> Whose onset made the rest audacious,
> Whereby they likewise have so well discharged
> Upon that hideous beast encroaching thus,
>
> And now must I with that poor strength I have,
> Resist so foul a foe in what I may.

In spite of the limitations of the form, and the greater limitations of Daniel's dramatic sense, *Cleopatra* is, in its quiet way, a masterpiece and the finest of all the closet dramas of the period. The verse is easy and accomplished; and, although there are no striking images or quotable lines, the account of Cleopatra's death is a remarkable piece of narrative verse:

> False flesh (saith she) and what dost thou conspire
> With Cæsar too, as thou wert none of ours,
> To work my shame, and hinder my desire?
> Wilt thou retain in closure of thy veins
> That enemy, base life, to let my good?
> No, know there is a greater power constrains
> Than can be counterchecked with fearful blood.
> For to the mind that's great, nothing seems great:
> And, seeing death to be the last of woes,
> And life lasting disgrace, which I shall get,
> What do I lose, that have but life to lose?

It was unlucky for Daniel that two greater poets should have written masterpieces on the same subject; but Dryden in the last act of *All for Love* made unacknowledged use of dozens of Daniel's actual phrases.

Daniel's later plays were written in the seventeenth century. *Philotas* (1605), another neo-Senecan tragedy, was actually performed by amateurs at Bath; but Daniel excused himself for the vulgarity of a performance by his shortage of money: "My necessity, I confess, hath driven me to do a thing unworthy of me, and much against my heart, in making the stage the speaker of my lines." The play got its author into trouble because it was thought to be a sympathetic portrayal of the ill-fated Earl of Essex. *Philotas* is certainly more dramatic than *Cleopatra*: there is a trial scene, a character dies on stage, and the language is more colloquial. But it would be absurd to suggest that it was a good acting play. Daniel himself recognized his limitations and spoke of his "misery, that whilst I should have written of the actions of men, I have been constrained to live with children."

Much more interesting were two pastoral plays, *The Queen's Arcadia* (1606) and *Hymen's Triumph* (1615), which earned the admiration of Coleridge on account of the singular purity of their style. Daniel avoided poetic diction and narrowly escaped the prosaic; but he did escape it, and in these plays his limited knowledge of the world was not the handicap it was in his tragedies. One example must suffice of the style of *Hymen's Triumph*. In this speech Thirsis discovers that a wounded boy is his long-lost Silvia:

> And art thou thus returned again to me?
> Art thou thy self that strange-delivered nymph?
> And didst thou come to tell me thine escape
> From death, to die before me? Had I not
> Enough to do, to wail reported harms
> But thou must come to bleed within my arms?
> Was not one death sufficient for my griefs
> But that thou must die twice? Why, thou wert dead
> To me before! Why? must thou die again?
> Ah, better had it been still to be lost
> Than thus to have been found! Yet better found,
> Though thus, than so lost as was thought before.

Daniel's most ambitious work, *The Civil Wars,* appeared first in 1595; but in later editions it was expanded to cover the whole period from the reign of Richard II to the end of the Wars of the Roses. This long narrative poem of almost epic proportions was criticized by contemporaries for its failure to describe the battles. This is not as serious a fault as might appear, for Daniel avoided martial scenes, not merely because he knew his own limitations, but because he was interested in causes and motives rather than in physical action. Another complaint, that he was "too much historian in verse," has more substance. He is tied too much, as Shakespeare and Drayton were not, to the facts of history. The poem comes alive in those passages where he dares to invent, or to embroider, the historical facts. The description of the entry into London of Richard and Bolingbroke (which Shakespeare clearly remembered when he wrote *Richard II* soon afterward) and the meditations of Richard in prison are both impressive; and here and there the sober, prosaic narrative is lit up by a striking image:

> And look, how Thames, enriched with many a flood,
> And goodly rivers (that have made their graves
> And buried both their names and all their good
> Within his greatness, to augment his waves)
> Glides on, with pomp of waters, unwithstood,
> Unto the ocean, which his tribute craves . . .

The penultimate line was quoted by Wordsworth in one of his sonnets. Unexciting as much of *The Civil Wars* is, it has enough sober political wisdom in it to make one understand why Coleridge should tell Lamb that "Thousands even of educated men would become more sensible, fitter to be members of Parliament or ministers, by reading Daniel." [2]

Daniel's most important work was still to come. He found a form best suited to his talents in *Musophilus*

---

[2] *Miscellaneous Criticism*, ed. T. M. Raysor (Cambridge, Mass.: Harvard University Press, 1936) p. 236.

and in the verse epistles addressed to various members of the nobility. He was able to express in them his deepest and most constant feelings—on the importance of poetry and on the importance of virtue. *Musophilus* (1599), dedicated to Fulke Greville, who had acted as his patron after he left the Countess of Pembroke's service, is in the form of a dialogue between Philocosmos, who regards poetry as a waste of time, unfitting people for the real world, and Musophilus, Daniel's own spokesman, who argues that literary fame lasts longer than any other and that in times of crisis the learned man is needed by the state. In any case, he cannot give up writing poetry:

> This is the thing that I was born to do,
> This is my scene, this part I must fulfill.

The poem ends with a magnificent passage on the potentialities of the English language as a medium for poetry, perhaps even in the New World:

> Or should we, careless, come behind the rest
> In power of words, that go before in worth,
> Whenas our accents equal to the best,
> Is able greater wonders to bring forth:
> When all that ever hotter spirits expressed
> Comes bettered by the patience of the North.
> And who, in time, knows whither we may vent
> The treasure of our tongue, to what strange shores
> This gain of our best glory shall be sent
> T'enrich unknowing Nations with our stores?
> What worlds in th'yet unformed Occident
> May come refined with th'accents that are ours.

He concludes that

> Those numbers wherewith Heaven and Earth are moved,
> Show weakness speaks in prose, but power in verse.

Although Daniel, like Greville, rejected poetic diction and all superfluous ornament, we never feel, as we do with Greville's verse treatises, that everything has been sacrificd to an unswerving didactic purpose. In his epistles Daniel clearly has a didactic purpose—not, of course, to the actual recipients who were assumed to possess the virtues of which he wrote—but he was also concerned with the expression of his ethical ideas in the most effective and graceful way. The basis of his moral position may be defined as stoicism tempered with Christianity.

Daniel manages to avoid the prosaic and the trite. The extraordinary purity of his diction, which, as Coleridge remarked, is less antiquated than Shakespeare's,[3] enabled him to use the language of prose without ceasing to write poetry. He was saved, partly by the dignity of his themes and partly by the superiority of Elizabethan English as a vehicle for poetry compared with the ordinary language of the early nineteenth century.

In writing to Sir Thomas Egerton, Daniel differentiates between law and justice, since the recipient, "Great Keeper of the State of Equity," endeavors to withdraw "Justice from out the tempests of the Law." In the epistle to Lord Henry Howard, Daniel writes on the desirability (as Hamlet put it) of not being Fortune's slave:

> And though sometimes th'event may fall amiss,
> Yet shall it still have honour for th'attempt,
> When craft begins with fear and ends with shame,
> And in the whole design perplexed is;
> Virtue, though luckless, yet shall scape contempt,
> And though it hath not hap, it shall have fame.

[3] *Table Talk*, March 15, 1834.

He exhorts his pupil Anne Clifford, who, years later, erected a tablet to his memory, to follow the example of her mother, who had sought to adorn

> That better part, the mansion of your mind,
> With all the richest furniture of worth . . .
> She tells you how that honour only is
> A goodly garment put on fair deserts,
> Wherein the smallest stain is greatest seen;
> And that it cannot grace unworthiness,
> But more apparent shows defective parts,
> How gay soever they are decked therein.

Better still are the lines addressed to the Earl of Southampton, Shakespeare's patron, who had been imprisoned for his part in the Essex conspiracy:

> It is not but the tempest that doth show
> The seaman's cunning: but the field that tries
> The captain's courage: and we come to know
> Best what men are in their worse jeopardies:
> For lo! how many have we seen to grow
> To high renown from lowest miseries,
> Out of the hands of death, and many a one
> T'have been undone, had they not been undone.

The favorite epistle of Wordsworth and Coleridge, both of whom quoted from it, is the one addressed to the Countess of Cumberland. It has the same nobility of tone as the others. Daniel describes the man "that of such a height hath built his mind," who looks down

> Upon these lower regions of turmoil!
> Where all the storms of passions mainly beat
> On flesh and blood; where honour, power, renown
> Are only gay afflictions, golden toil.

He concludes that

> unless above himself he can
> Erect himself, how poor a thing is man!

Impressive as much of this poem is, it suffers in some stanzas, by comparison with the others, from some disjointed rhythms and awkward enjambments.

Daniel wrote very few lyrics — unless some of the songs set to music by his brother are by him — but those he did write are unexpectedly light and charming. They include one or two in the later plays and masques, an exquisite version of Tasso's chorus on the Golden Age, and the dialogue between Ulysses and the Syren, which (as Joan Rees says) "presents a beautifully controlled and supple lyric surface beneath which subtle thoughts and fine shades of meaning move and interweave."

One other work of Daniel's remains to be mentioned. In 1602 Thomas Campion published his *Observations on the Art of English Poesie,* in which he advocated the abandonment of rhyme and the use of classical meters. Twenty years earlier Sidney, Spenser, Harvey, and Greville had all experimented without success in classical meters. They had some excuse because at that time none of the greatest Elizabethan poetry had been written. Campion himself was already the author of some excellent songs, and he was to become the most consistently good lyric writer of his age, so that his thesis was a strange one. Daniel, who had avoided blank verse even in *Cleopatra,* wrote *A Defence of Rhyme* (1603) in reply to Campion. It is notable for its polite and urbane tone, for its avoidance of mere polemic, and for its shrewd demonstration that "rhyme is the fittest harmony of words that comports with our language." After Sidney's *Defence* it is easily the best Elizabethan critical essay, wider in scope than its title might suggest.

MICHAEL DRAYTON

Michael Drayton (1563–1631), a Warwickshire man
like Shakespeare, was a dedicated poet who never once
deviated into prose and only once into drama. He developed late, and his earliest volumes, *The Harmony of
the Church* (1591), *Idea, the Shepherd's Garland* (1593),
and *Idea's Mirror* (1594), show few signs of poetic
promise and *Piers Gaveston* and *Matilda,* not much more.
But Drayton gradually shed most of his weaknesses,
and he himself became so dissatisfied with his early
work that he radically revised it in later editions. The
revisions, however, were not always improvements. His
first good poem, the mythological *Endimion and Phoebe*
(1595), written in well-turned heroic couplets and dis-
playing a freshness and delicacy he did not often excel,
was rewritten nine years later as a dull and ponderous
narrative, *The Man in the Moon.*

But if one reads his sonnets in the various editions
between 1594 and 1619 one is struck by his elimination
of the weakest sonnets in *Idea's Mirror,* by his improvement of others, and above all by the fact that the new
additions to the sequence become progressively better
so that the final version of *Idea* contains some of the best
sonnets of the period outside Shakespeare's sequence.
Indeed, there is good reason to believe that Drayton
learned from Shakespeare to come closer to colloquial
speech and to the expression of natural human feelings.

Drayton's early sonnets give the impression of being
mere exercises, an attempt to be in the fashion rather
than the expression of genuine experience. Here is a
typical example:

Three sorts of serpents do resemble thee:
That dangerous eye-killing cockatrice,
Th'enchanting syren, which doth so entice,
The weeping crocodile—these vile pernicious three.
The basilisk his nature takes from thee,
Who for my life in secret wait dost lie,
And to my heart send'st poison from thine eye:
Thus do I feel the pain, the cause yet cannot see.
Fair maid no more, but mermaid be thy name,
Who with thy sweet alluring harmony
Hast played the thief, and stolen my heart from me,
And, like a tyrant, mak'st my grief thy game.
   The crocodile who, when thou hast me slain,
   Lament'st my death with tears of thy disdain.

Apart from the staleness of the imagery and the total unreality of the whole sonnet, it is badly constructed; and it contains alexandrines at the end of the first two quatrains, but not at the end of the third.

In the later sonnets the language became simpler and more direct, the imagery more original and also more appropriate, the lines more melodious; and the poems give the impression, which may be an illusion, of genuine feeling. Even when Drayton was expressing a poetic commonplace—in this case the immortalizing power of poetry—he makes of it something fresh:

How many paltry, foolish, painted things,
That now in coaches trouble every street,
Shall be forgotten, whom no poet sings,
Ere they be well wrapped in their winding sheet!
Where I to thee eternity shall give,
When nothing else remaineth of these days,
And queens hereafter shall be glad to live
Upon the alms of thy superfluous praise.
Virgins and matrons reading these my rhymes
Shall be so much delighted with thy story,
That they shall grieve they lived not in these times,

To have seen thee, their sex's only glory:
  So shalt thou fly above the vulgar throng,
  Still to survive in my immortal song.

The scorn in the opening lines expressed by the heap of adjectives and the verb "trouble" and the wonderful phrasing of l. 8 show how far Drayton had traveled from his early looseness of expression. Best of all is the "wonderful dry-eyed sonnet" (as Oliver Elton called it) in which Drayton says farewell to the woman he had loved for so many years.[4]

Since there's no help, come let us kiss and part.
Nay, I have done: you get no more of me,
And I am glad, yea glad with all my heart,
That thus so cleanly I myself can free.
Shake hands for ever, cancel all our vows,
And when we meet at any time again,
Be it not seen in either of our brows
That we one jot of former love retain.
Now at the last gasp of Love's latest breath,
When, his pulse failing, Passion speechless lies,
When Faith is kneeling by his bed of death,
And Innocence is closing up his eyes,
  Now, if thou would'st, when all have given him over,
  From death to life thou might'st him yet recover.

This sonnet, as dramatic as the best of Sidney and Shakespeare, depends for its effect on the extraordinary simplicity of its diction—the first three lines consist entirely of monosyllables—on the reticence, restraint, and precision with which the poet's grief is expressed, and on the vivid image in the sestet, with its successful personifications.

[4] The "Idea" of the sonnets was Anne Goodere, later Lady Rainsford; and to judge from the poem written by Drayton on his deathbed, they were afterward reconciled.

Drayton's most ambitious poem was *Mortimeriados* (1596), revised seven years later as *The Barons' Wars*. The earlier version was written in rhyme royal, the later version in ottava rima, the stanza used by Daniel in *The Civil Wars*. Drayton explained in his preface the reasons for the change. He felt that ottava rima was the most complete and best-proportioned stanza, partly because it did not have the two couplets at the end. Drayton eliminated most of the weaknesses of the earlier version. In the stanzas describing Edward II in prison, for example, he changed the lines

> The croaking raven's hideous voice he hears,
> Which through the castle sounds with deadly yells

to the more satisfactory

> The ominous raven often he doth hear,
> Whose croaking him of following honour tells.

The conventionally "envious dog" becomes the "howling dog"; the epithet "buzzing" is transferred from the night crow to the screech owl; and Drayton adds a splendid line:

> Of wandering helpless in far foreign realms.

The theme of the poem was the same as Marlowe's *Edward II*, published in 1594; and although Drayton has nothing to equal Marlowe's scenes of the deposition and murder of Edward, he quite properly concentrated on the story of Mortimer and Isabella. He avoids Daniel's mistake of keeping too close to the facts of history; and we can tell from the remark he quotes about Daniel—that "his manner better fitted prose"—and from his own practice, that he thought a more poetic diction was appropriate to historical epic. As a narrative poet he was much better than Daniel: he gets on with the story and avoids philosophizing about it.

Drayton's method can be seen at its best in the last canto, where the passion of Isabella for Mortimer, just before his overthrow, is conveyed indirectly by the splendidly sensuous description of her room and more directly in the description of their love making:

> Her loose hair looked like gold (O word too base!
> Nay, more than sin, but so to name her hair)
> Declining, as to kiss her fairer face,
> No word is fair enough for thing so fair,
> Nor never was there epithet could grace
> That, by much praising, which we much impair:
>   And where the pen fails, pencils cannot show it;
>   Only the soul may be supposed to know it.
>
> She laid her fingers on his manly cheek,
> The gods' pure sceptres, and the darts of love,
> That with their touch might make a tiger meek,
> Or might great Atlas from his seat remove;
> So white, so soft, so delicate, so sleek,
> As she had worn a lily for a glove,
>   As might beget life, where was never none,
>   And put a spirit into the hardest stone.

The Barons' Wars was the best historical narrative poem of the period and, as it was reprinted eight times during Drayton's lifetime, one of the most popular. But Elizabethan readers had an insatiable appetite for historical information, as can be seen from the popularity of the pedestrian prose chroniclers Holinshed and Stow; from the extraordinary vogue of *The Mirror for Magistrates;* and from the large number of English history plays on subjects ranging from the legendary Leir to the reign of Elizabeth's immediate predecessor, Mary.

The process of painstaking revision can be followed also in Drayton's pastoral poems. He probably adopted the eclogue form because of the reputation of *The Shepherd's Calendar,* but he does not have a clearly discernible didactic purpose. The pastorals, as revised, contain some charming passages of description and some excellent songs. One of the best ("Gorbo, as thou cam'st this way") first appeared in *England's Helicon* (1600). But Drayton's best pastorals were written in his old age. *The Shepherd's Sirena* (1627) and *The Muses' Elizium* (1630) display a lyric grace that is absent from his early poems. Decorative, colorful, and melodious as they are, they are never likely to be popular because of the thinness of content and ultimate remoteness from reality. They are, not in a derogatory sense, escapist poems.

The mention of these later pastorals shows how impossible it is to confine one's attention to the poems written by Drayton in the reign of Elizabeth. All his most enduring work was written later, with the exception perhaps, of *England's Heroical Epistles* (1597), suggested by Ovid's *Heroides,* but, unlike the latter's, the epistles were supposed to be exchanged not between characters of mythology, but between personages of recent English history. The *Heroical Epistles* are written in closed couplets, and they are much more similar to those of Waller and Dryden than they are to the couplets written by Drayton's own contemporaries. The same thing is true of the later elegies.

Drayton tried his hand at satire; but *The Owl* (1604) was notoriously obscure even to his contemporaries, who interpreted it in different ways. Roger, in Beaumont and Fletcher's *The Scornful Lady,* complains that he has

been jilted by a lady after he had gone to the trouble
of explaining *The Owl* to her.

Drayton's masterpieces are *Nymphidia* (1627), a fairy
poem worthy to stand beside *A Midsummer Night's
Dream, The Ballad of Agincourt* (1606), two or three of
the odes published in 1606, almost Horatian in their
grace and concision, and the song in *The Shepherds'
Sirena*. Written in a tripping meter with alternate
feminine rhymes, this song contains some delightfully
extravagant conceits and suggests, more successfully than
"The Brook" of Tennyson, the noise and movement of
the stream:

> Near to the silver Trent
>   Sirena dwelleth:
> She to whom Nature lent
>   All that excelleth:
> By which the Muses late
>   And the neat Graces,
> Have for their greater state
>   Taken their places:
> Twisting an anadem
>   Wherewith to crown her,
> As it belonged to them
>   Most to renown her.
>
> The fishes in the flood
>   When she doth angle,
> For the hook strive a good
>   Them to entangle;
> And leaping on the land
>   From the clear water,
> Their scales upon the sand
>   Lavishly scatter;
> Therewith to pave the mould
>   Whereon she passes,
> So herself to behold
>   As in her glasses.

Drayton, however, regarded as his masterpiece the poem on which he spent some twenty years. *Poly-olbion* (1612, 1622) is a huge topographical description of England, some 12,000 lines long. This is a fine reflection of Drayton's patriotism, and it exhibits his love of the countryside and of its historical and antiquarian associations. It contains some lovely descriptive passages, especially in those books concerned with the counties he knew best, Warwickshire and Derbyshire. But it would be vain to deny that, in spite of the attractiveness of parts of the poem, its total effect is one of monotony. Drayton called his books "Songs," but much of the verse is flat and prosaic; and the poem lacks inevitably a narrative drive or the interest of a connected argument. It ambles along pleasantly enough, and one can admire what Drayton calls his "strange Herculean toil" without being fully convinced that verse was the right medium.

Drayton wrote the whole poem in rhymed alexandrines with a caesura in the middle of each line. This means that the reader, accustomed to pentameters, splits each line into two, and the effect is disastrous. Here, for example, are some lines describing the River Severn:

> Now Sabrine, as a queen, miraculously fair,
> Is absolutely placed in her imperial chair,
> Of crystal richly wrought, that gloriously did shine,
> Her grace becoming well a creature so divine:
> And as her godlike self, so glorious was her throne,
> In which himself to sit great Neptune had been known.

It is clear from the preface to the poem and from a long digression in Book XXI, where he complains that good poets are not properly respected in the reign of

James I, that Drayton felt he had outgrown his former popularity. Donne and the metaphysicals were all the rage. The reading public preferred witty conceits in short lyrics to long ambitious poems in which one had to search for the more poetic passages or be content with a versified guidebook. "At this time," said Drayton, "verses are wholly deduced to chambers, and nothing esteemed in this lunatic age, but what is kept in cabinets and must only pass by transcription."

But it should not be thought that Drayton belonged entirely to the past. Although he had links with Spenser and Sidney, some of his work looks forward to a period when the metaphysicals were no longer in fashion, after the Restoration.

Suggested Reading

There is a good selection of Daniel's works, *Poems and A Defence of Rhyme,* by A. C. Sprague (Cambridge, Mass.: Harvard Univ. Press, 1930). *The Civil Wars,* edited by L. Michel (New Haven, Conn: Yale Univ. Press, 1958), is the first volume of a projected edition of the complete works. Another is being prepared by John Buxton for the Clarendon Press. *Samuel Daniel,* by Joan Rees (Liverpool Univ. Press, 1964) is the only full study of the poet.

The standard edition of Drayton's works is by J. W. Hebel, K. Tillotson, and B. H. Newdigate (Oxford: Blackwell, 1931-41). There are selections by C. Brett (Oxford: Clarendon Press, 1907) and J. Buxton (London: Routledge and Kegan Paul, 1953). *Michael Drayton, A Critical Study* by Oliver Elton (Edinburgh: Constable, 1905) and *Michael Drayton and His Circle* by B. H. Newdigate (Oxford: Blackwell, 1941) are both valuable.

V
Miscellanies, Song Books and Some Other Poets

There were a dozen or more verse anthologies published in the reign of Elizabeth I, and they are of several different kinds. Some were rather dictionaries of quotations, arranged according to subject, such as *England's Parnassus* (1600) and *Belvedere* (1600). Others purported to be the work of a single author, such as Gascoigne's *A Hundreth Sundry Flowers* (1573), Breton's *The Bower of Delights* (1591), and the collection, ascribed by an unscrupulous publisher to Shakespeare, entitled *The Passionate Pilgrim* (1599). The anthology that maintains the highest level is *England's Helicon*

(1600), a collection of pastoral poetry for which the editor relied mainly on published work by Sidney, Spenser, Greene, Drayton, Lodge, Munday, Chettle, and others. But the two most valuable anthologies—because they were collections of hitherto unpublished poems— were *The Phoenix Nest* (1593) and Davison's *Poetical Rhapsody* (1602). The former contains poems by Lodge, Ralegh, Watson, Dyer, Peele, and others. Five of the authors were at Oxford at about the same time, and there is some slight evidence that the contributors were loosely associated.

The Phoenix Nest opens oddly with a prose eulogy of Leicester, followed by three elegies on Sidney, by Roydon, Ralegh, and Dyer; and, from a passage in Roydon's, it looks as though the title of the anthology was intended to imply that poetry, which had died with Sidney, would rise, like a phoenix, from its ashes. Certainly, if one compares *The Phoenix Nest* with *A Gorgeous Gallery of Gallant Inventions* or *The Paradise of Dainty Devices,* one can see that the verse of nearly all the contributors was more polished and sophisticated than in the previous collections, and that the poets had learned from the new poetry of Spenser and Sidney. The best poems are Ralegh's, especially the elegy on Sidney, a beautifully composed tribute that expresses a national, rather than a personal, grief; but several of the anonymous poems are impressive, including a poem addressed to Night, which in less skillful hands might have reminded us of Pyramus and Thisbe:

O Night, O jealous Night, repugnant to my pleasures,

and a poem written in an original and complex fourteen-line stanza:

Sweet violets, Love's paradise, that spread
   Your gracious odours, which you couched bear
    Within your paly faces,
Upon the gentle wing of some calm-breathing wind
   That plays amidst the plain,
   If by the favour of propitious stars you gain
Such grace as in my lady's bosom place to find,
    Be proud to touch those places;
   And when her warmth your moisture forth doth wear,
Whereby her dainty parts are sweetly fed,
   Your honours of the flowery meads, I pray,
You pretty daughters of the earth and sun,
   With mild and seemly breathing straight display
My bitter sighs that have my heart undone.

Davison's *Poetical Rhapsody* is even better: it contains
some good poems by Ralegh, Sir John Davies, Sidney,
and Campion, a large number of anonymous poems, and
groups of poems by Francis Davison, the compiler, and
his brother Walter. Most of Davison's own poems are
accomplished, but lacking in originality; but Walter was
a fine poet and well deserved his place in the collection.
Here, for example, is the first stanza of "A Dialogue
Between Him and His Heart":

At her fair hands how have I grace entreated,
    With prayers oft repeated
    Yet still my love is thwarted!
Heart, let her go, for she'll not be converted.
    Say, shall she go?
    Oh no, no, no, no, no;
She is most fair, though she be marble-hearted.

He maintains, gracefully and effortlessly, this difficult
rhyme scheme through five more stanzas.

Walter Davison may also be responsible for some of
the anonymous poems, several of which display the same
elegance:

My love in her attire doth show her wit,
  It doth so well become her.
For every season she hath dressings fit,
  For Winter, Spring and Summer.
    No beauty she doth miss
      When all her robes are on:
    But Beauty's self she is,
      When all her robes are gone.

SONG BOOKS

Many of the best Elizabethan lyrics are to be found in
the song books of the period. The composers, who included Byrd, Morley, Dowland, and Gibbons, sometimes
set poems that had been previously published and sometimes lyrics that were circulating in manuscript. Some
of them, however, such as Thomas Campion, wrote their
own words.

In the madrigals the words are less important than
the music, and they can hardly stand alone, as, for
example, these verses set by Thomas Morley:

Sing we and chant it,
While love doth grant it.
Not long youth lasteth,
And old age hasteth.
Now is best leisure
To take our pleasure.
All things invite us
Now to delight us.
Hence, Care, be packing;
No mirth be lacking;
Let spare no treasure
To live in pleasure.

The songs for the lute are more significant as poetry.
William Byrd set Dyer's poem "My mind to me a king-

dom is" and the anonymous song, afterward included in *England's Helicon,* "What pleasure have great princes." John Dowland's lutanist songs include some of the finest Elizabethan lyrics, such as "I saw my lady weep" and the exquisite "Weep you no more, sad fountains":

Weep you no more, sad fountains;
　　What need you flow so fast?
Look how the snowy mountains
　　Heaven's sun doth gently waste.
But my sun's heavenly eyes
　　View not your weeping,
　　That now lies sleeping
Softly, now softly lies
　　Sleeping.

Sleep is a reconciling,
　　A rest that peace begets.
Doth not the sun rise smiling
　　When fair at ev'n he sets?
Rest you, then, rest, sad eyes,
　　Melt not in weeping,
　　While she lies sleeping
Softly, now softly lies
　　Sleeping.

The poetical level of Dowland's collections is equaled only by those of Robert Jones, of which the poems are anonymous, and those of Thomas Campion.

Campion, who was a doctor of medicine, first appeared in print in the piratical edition of *Astrophel and Stella*; but it was not until 1601, when he was thirty-four, that he collaborated with Philip Rosseter in *A Book of Airs,* of which he was the composer of half the settings and probably the author of all the poems. He published many songs later, and he wrote some of the best

Jacobean masques, but he never excelled the poems in this first collection, which includes the famous "When to her lute Corinna sings," a fine adaptation of Catullus:

> My sweetest Lesbia, let us live and love,
> And though the sager sort our deeds reprove,
> Let us not weigh them. Heaven's great lamps do dive
> Into their west, and straight again revive,
> But soon as once set is our little light,
> Then must we sleep one ever-during night;

a superbly modulated poem that seems almost to dictate its own tune:

> Follow your saint, follow with accents sweet;
> Haste you, sad notes, fall at her flying feet;
> There, wrapped in cloud of sorrow, pity move,
> And tell the ravisher of my soul I perish for her love.
> But if she scorns my never-ceasing pain,
> Then burst with sighing in her sight and ne'er return
> again;

a charming pastoral:

> I care not for these Ladies
>   That must be wooed and prayed;
> Give me kind Amarillis,
>   The wanton country maid;

and ten or twelve others that are equally successful. It is no exaggeration to say that Campion maintains a higher level than any other English songwriter.

It is very strange, therefore, that after writing this first collection, Campion should have argued against the use of rhyme in his *Observations on the Art of English Poesie*. Undeterred by the failures of Spenser and Sidney, he urged his fellow poets to revert to the use of the unrhymed verse of the Greeks and Romans. He provided some experiments in classical meters, and one of them is more successful than Spenser's or Sidney's:

> Rose-cheeked Laura, come
> Sing thou smoothly with thy beauty's
> Silent music, either other
> Sweetly gracing.

But in his later books of songs he seems to have tacitly recognized his mistake, for they all use rhymed verse.

Campion displays an extraordinary variety in his published songs, both in form and content. He uses many different stanza forms and numerous different meters, and some of his metrical effects are exquisite. One poem, for example, suggests the rhythm of a dance:

> Kind are her answers,
> But her performance keeps no day;
> Breaks time, as dancers
> From their own music when they stray.
> All her free favours
> And smooth words wing my hopes in vain.
> O! did ever voice so sweet but only feign?
> Can true love yield such delay,
> Converting joy to pain?

Nor is it true, as some critics have complained, that his verse is lacking in magic and in the strangeness that Bacon regarded as an essential of beauty. One of Campion's earliest poems, "Hark, all you ladies that do sleep," and one of the later songs in the *Third Book of Airs* (c. 1617):

> Thrice toss these oaken ashes in the air,
> Thrice sit thou mute in this enchanted chair,

are sufficient to dispose of that criticism. He lacks, it is true, the wit and originality of the best of the metaphysical poets; but he is in some ways a better love poet because his experience is more universal than Donne's or Suckling's. He could express the pangs of unreturned love more convincingly than most Elizabethan son-neteers; he knew the beauty that was "but a painted hell"; and sometimes his scorn at double-dealing and faithlessness pours out in long impetuous lines:

Think'st thou to seduce me then with words that have
  no meaning?
Parrots so can learn to prate, our speech by pieces gleaning:
Nurses teach their children so about the time of weaning.

But Campion is also a poet of happy love, as when he attacks jealousy and proclaims that love's service is per-fect freedom:

True love will yet be free,
In spite of jealousy.

SIR WALTER RALEGH

Ralegh (1552–1618) was a soldier, a sailor, an ex-plorer, a courtier, a statesman, a philosopher, and a historian; and his literary work was the byproduct of a life devoted to public affairs. Some of his verse, indeed, was written with the practical object of furthering his career.

Most of his poetry has been lost, and not all the poems ascribed to him are certainly his. One of his poems was published in 1576. His *Cynthia* was praised by Spenser in *Colin Clout's Come Home Again*; and about the same time Puttenham declared that "for ditty and amo-rous ode, I find Sir Walter Ralegh's vein the most lofty, insolent and passionate." [1] It is probable that Ralegh's contributions to *The Phoenix Nest* and *England's Helicon* were written at this time.

Most of these early poems are written in end-stopped pentameters. Ralegh uses a great deal of repetition and antithesis; he frequently omits the definite article; he begins many of his lines with a stressed syllable; and he sometimes uses assonance in place of a feminine rhyme. These characteristics, though not peculiar to Ralegh's verse, may help to authenticate his authorship of anonymous poems in *The Phoenix Nest*.

The best of these early poems are the elegy on Sidney, of which we have already spoken, the splendid sonnet in praise of *The Faerie Queene,* and "As you came from the Holy Land," which begins as a simple ballad and ends with the haunting music of the stanzas in which sexual desire is contrasted with the love of God:

His desire is a dureless content,
　　And a trustless joy:
He is won with a world of despair,
　　And is lost with a toy.

Of womenkind such indeed is the love,
　　Or the word love abused,
Under which many childish desires
　　And conceits are excused.

But true love is a durable fire
　　In the mind ever burning,
Never sick, never old, never dead,
　　From itself never turning.

It is possible that some of the poems included in *The Phoenix Nest* were part of the *Cynthia* mentioned by

[1] *The Arte of English Poesie* (1589).

Spenser and Harvey. The refrain of "Farewell to the Court"—"Of all which past, the sorow onely stays"— was quoted by Ralegh in the "21st and last Book of the Ocean's Love to Cynthia" written some years later; and several other poems were clearly written about the Queen. This stanza in an anonymous poem, very much in Ralegh's style, must refer to Elizabeth:

O eyes that pierce our hearts without remorse!
O hairs of right that wears a royal crown!
O hands that conquer more than Caesar's force!
O wit that turns huge kingdoms upside down!

In another poem Ralegh writes of one that "Kings have not obtained" and of himself as one who

sunk in search to gain that shore
Where many a Prince had perished before.

Spenser spoke of *Cynthia* as "the music of the summer's nightingale," and doubtless he saw more than the few poems that have survived. But there is something of a mystery. When Ralegh composed his longest and most impressive poem in 1592 he called it "The 21st and last book of the Ocean's to Cynthia," although it is difficult to believe that he had actually written twenty books before.

The manuscript, in the poet's hand, is not the first draft of the poem; but it is in a rough and unfinished state. Quatrains are left uncompleted; there are unrhymed lines, sentences that break off in the middle, and considerable discontinuity. But these flaws are less serious than might be supposed. Despite the fragmentary nature of the poem, it is a remarkable achievement as an exploration by Ralegh of his complex feelings about the

Queen, for its originality of cadence and metrical effect, and also for the precision of its imagery. Ralegh describes himself as gleaning "broken ears with miser's hands"; his heart is like "a body violently slain," which retains its warmth; Cynthia "sent her memory,"

> More strong than were ten thousand ships of war.

His woe is compared to the moss, which,

> Having compassion of unburied bones,
> Cleaves to mischance of unrepaired loss.

He compares himself to one who is

> Alone, forsaken, friendless on the shore,
> With many wounds, with death's cold pangs embraced,
> Writes in the dust, as one that could no more.

He declares that his lines are now no more than a murmuring in Cynthia's ears:

> Like to a falling stream which passing slow
> Is wont to nourish sleep and quietness;

and he speaks of

> The broken monuments of my great desires.

Even more original than the imagery is the rhythmical virtuosity, as, for example, near the end of the poem, where there is a sudden change of mood and music:

> She is gone, she is lost! She is found, she is ever fair.
> Sorrow draws weakly, where love draws not too;
> Woe's cries sound nothing but only in love's ear;
> Do then by dying what life cannot do.

Cynthia is not Ralegh's most perfect poem, but it is the one that, despite its obvious imperfections and obscurities, give us the best idea of his genius.

Ralegh seems to have written little verse after 1592, but what there is shows considerable variety. "The Lie" is a splendid piece of invective in which Ralegh exposes one by one the evils in court, in church, and in society; he tells his soul:

> Say to the Court it glows
>   And shines like rotten wood;
> Say to the Church it shows
>   What's good, and doth no good:
> If Church and Court reply,
> Then give them both the lie.

Another poem, "The Passionate Man's Pilgrimage," is so different in style from all of Ralegh's other verse that Professor Philip Edwards is inclined to deny his authorship. But Ralegh's style varies considerably in the poems that have survived; there is some evidence that he did write it when under sentence of death; and the use of a serious quibble, though uncharacteristic, is a favorite and effective device of Elizabethan poets, including the greatest:

> From thence to heaven's bribeless hall,
> Where no corrupted voices brawl,
> No conscience molten into gold,
> Nor forged accusers bought and sold,
> No cause deferred, nor vain-spent journey,
> For there Christ is the King's Attorney,
> Who pleads for all without degrees,
> And he hath angels, but no fees.

Ralegh had reason to hate Coke, the King's Attorney, who had called him "the most vile and execrable traitor that ever lived" in a trial that was certainly framed. The difference in style cannot prove that Ralegh was not the author; for, in an earlier poem, beginning "Our passions are most like to floods and streams," he had written in a style that is more like that of a Caroline than an Elizabethan poet:

> Silence in love bewrays more woe
>   Than words, though ne'er so witty;
> A beggar that is dumb, ye know,
>   Deserveth double pity.
>
> Then misconceive not, dearest heart,
>   My true, though secret, passion:
> He smarteth most that hides his smart,
>   And sues for no compassion.

So much of Ralegh's verse has been lost that it is difficult to judge him as a poet; but, because there was no social stigma attached to the publication of prose, his prose works are considerable in quantity. At his best, he was among the greatest writers of his age. His splendid account of the last fight of *The Revenge* is superior in force and epic grandeur to Tennyson's poem on the same subject ("The Revenge"). The cadence of the following sentence illustrates the power and beauty of the prose, which, however, are not the result of a deliberate striving for seductive rhythms, as those of Landor and De Quincey sometimes seem to be:

> What became of the body, whether it was buried in the sea or on the land we know not: the comfort that remaineth to his friends is, that he hath ended his life honourably in respect of the reputation won to his nation and country, and of the same to his posterity, and that being dead, he hath not outlived his own honour.

Ralegh's account of *The Discovery of Guiana* (1596)— another work of propaganda—contains some vivid descriptive passages; and his unfinished *History of the*

World (1614), written in prison in the seventeenth century, is a superb epic chronicle of the working of God in history. In all three works, and particularly in the *History,* Ralegh displays a mastery of prose rhythm that has seldom been equaled and never, perhaps, excelled. The man who wrote this famous passage on death was a consummate artist:

> It is therefore Death alone that can suddenly make man to know himself. He tells the proud and insolent, that they are but abjects, and humbles them at the instant; makes them cry, complain and repent, yea even to hate their forepassed happiness. He takes the account of the rich, and proves him a beggar, which hath interest in nothing, but in the gravel that fills his mouth. He holds a glass before the eyes of the most beautiful, and makes them see therein their deformity and rottenness; and they acknowledge it. O eloquent, just and mighty Death! Whom none could advise, thou hast persuaded; what none hath dared, thou hast done; and whom all the world hath flattered, thou only hast cast out of the world, and despised: thou hast drawn together all the far-stretched greatness, all the pride, cruelty and ambition of man, and covered it all over with these two narrow words, *Hic Jacet.*

GEORGE CHAPMAN

The early volumes of George Chapman (1560–1634) gave no promise of the translator of Homer, who spoke out loud and bold and enchanted the young Keats. *The Shadow of Night* (1594) is crabbed, overintellectual, pedantic, and obscure. Chapman despised the general reader and told Matthew Royden that if poetry were as lucid as oratory, "it would be the plain way to barbarism." He admitted, indeed, that "obscurity in diction and indigested conceits" was pedantic; but he claimed that his own obscurity was justified by the difficulty and profundity of his subject. His subject matter was certainly difficult, but his obscurity was partly due to a failure of communication. Here and there, only, are short passages in which the meaning comes across, as in the famous lines in which Chapman praises the night as the inspirer of poetry:

> Come consecrate with me to sacred Night
> Your whole endeavours, and detest the light.
> Sweet Peace's richest crown is made of stars,
> Most certain guides of honoured mariners:
> No pen can anything eternal write
> That is not steeped in humour of the night.

To the last couplet Shakespeare replied through the mouth of Berowne in *Love's Labour's Lost*.

Chapman gradually developed a less obscure style, as he was bound to do when he began to write for the stage toward the end of the century. Meanwhile, in *Ovid's Banquet of Sense* (1595) he produced a kind of narrative poem, intended apparently as a neoplatonic reply to such erotic poems as *Venus and Adonis* and *Hero and Leander,* though the author of *The Art of Love* is a strange choice of hero for a poem on such a subject. The same volume contains a short sonnet sequence for his mistress, Philosophy, and it was designed as a counterblast to the sequences addressed to mistresses of flesh and blood. The last sonnet is an attack on a contemporary dramatist, thought by some critics to be Shakespeare.

Chapman's third book was a continuation of Marlowe's *Hero and Leander;*[2] and, inspired by

[2] See p. 136ff.

> his free soul, whose living subject stood
> Up to the chin in the Pierean flood,

Chapman contrived to write a comparatively lucid poem of considerable power. It lacks both the wit and sensuous beauty of Marlowe's opening; it is written in a totally different tone, being more moralistic and less sympathetic to the lovers; but presumably if Marlowe had lived to complete the poem he too would have adopted a rather different style for the tragic ending. Chapman's narrative is surprisingly successful. He had by now begun to write for the stage and to translate Homer, and both occupations would necessitate a less obscure style than he had used in his early poems.

The first two installments of Chapman's translation of the *Iliad* were published in 1598; the complete translation was not finished until 1611, and the *Odyssey* appeared complete four years later. The translation of the *Iliad* is written in fourteeners, presumably because Chapman felt they were closer to Homeric hexameters than heroic couplets would have been, though in *The Shadow of Night* he had spoken of Latin hexameters as "those strange garments" and argued that the English Muse prefers "Our native robes . . . English heroics." In his translation of the *Odyssey* he reverted to his earlier opinion. Most modern readers find fourteeners unsatisfactory—Chapman had a precedent in Golding's translation of Ovid—because the line tends to break into two unequal parts, giving the effect of ballad meter. Here, for example, is Chapman's version of one of the great moments of the *Iliad*, Hector's farewell to Andromache:

> And such a stormy day shall come, in mind and soul I
> know,

When sacred Troy shall shed her towers for tears of
overthrow;
When Priam, all his birth and power, shall in those tears
be drowned.
But neither Troy's posterity so much my soul doth
wound,
Priam, nor Hecuba herself, nor all my brother's woes,
Who, though so many and so good, must all be food for
foes,
As thy sad state; when some rude Greek shall lead thee
weeping hence,
These free days clouded, and a night of captive violence
Loading thy temples, out of which thine eyes must never
see,
But spin the Greek wives webs of task, and their fetch-
water be.

This meter, tolerable in short extracts, becomes fatally
monotonous in the long run; and Chapman was wise to
abandon it in his translation of the *Odyssey*. But in both
poems he was led into frequent awkwardnesses in his
search for a rhyme, and he lacks the clarity and direct-
ness of the original. Chapman boasted that Homer had
appeared to him in a vision, encouraging him to the
task of translation, filling his bosom (as Homer said)

With such a flood of soul that thou wert fain,
With acclamations of her rapture then,
To vent it to the echoes of the vale . . .
And I, invisibly, went prompting thee
To those fair greens where thou didst English me.

Despite this claim to inspiration and Chapman's conviction that his Homer was his masterpiece, despite, indeed, Keats' enthusiasm, Chapman's best work is to be
found in the plays written in the seventeenth century
—*Bussy D'Ambois* and its sequel, and, more surprisingly, two brilliant comedies, *All Fools* and *The*

Widow's Tears—and in a haunting and strange poem entitled *Euthymiae Raptus: or The Tears of Peace.*

SIR JOHN DAVIES

Sir John Davies (1569–1626), who should not be confused with the less interesting John Davies of Hereford, wrote all his best poetry in the reign of Elizabeth before his duties as M.P. diverted his energies. He began unpromisingly with a collection of scurrilous epigrams and then emerged as a considerable poet with *Orchestra* (1596) and *Nosce Teipsum* (1599). His acrostic *Hymns to Astraea* (1599), his name for the Queen, although an amazing tour de force, are of less importance; and the poems included in Davison's *Poetical Rhapsody* are also of minor interest.

Orchestra, "This sudden, rash, half-capreol of my wit," as Davies called it in his dedication to Richard Martin, was written in fifteen days in 1594. In the second edition the ending was changed, partly because the praise of contemporary poets was no longer topical and partly because Davies had quarreled with Martin. The poem describes how Antinous, one of Penelope's suitors, defends dancing against her objections, on the grounds that order was brought out of chaos in the dance; that the stars in their courses, the sun, and the planets are all engaged in a dance; that speech itself consists of the moving of the air in a dance; that dancing was instituted by love; that the sea, the rivers, and even the flowers obey the rules of the dance; and that all the arts are based on dancing. What finally convinces Penelope, however, is a magic mirror in which she beholds Queen

Elizabeth and her maids of honor engaged in dancing. Although the poem leads up to this compliment to the Queen, it is much more universal in scope than its last section would suggest: for Davies' conception of dancing embodies a whole philosophy of life and embraces the physical universe as well as human relationships.

Davies writes with great gusto, gaiety, and charm, and at its best his verse is singularly beautiful:

> For lo! the sea that fleets about the land,
>   And like a girdle clips her solid waist,
> Music and measure both doth understand;
>   For his great crystal eye is always cast
>   Up to the moon, and on her fixed fast;
> And as she danceth in her pallid sphere,
> So danceth he about the centre here.

Nosce Teipsum, written after Davies had been expelled from the Middle Temple for his attack on Martin, is a philosophical poem of a more orthodox kind than *Orchestra.* The first part is concerned with the limitations of human knowledge, the danger of curiosity—the Fall being caused by it—and our ignorance of ourselves:

> We seek to know the moving of each sphere,
>   And the strange cause of th'ebbs and floods of Nile;
> But of that clock within our breasts we bear,
>   The subtle motions we forget the while.

> We that acquaint ourselves with every zone,
>   And pass both tropics, and behold both poles,
> When we come home are to ourselves unknown,
>   And unacquainted still with our own souls.

The second and longer part of the poem is an attempt to prove the immortality of the soul. Davies argues from the fact that man desires knowledge that cannot be satisfied in this life, from the way in which the soul aspires to God, and, since every human desire has a real object, from the general desire for immortality. As T. S. Eliot pointed out, Davies did not have a philosophical mind: "he was primarily a poet with a gift of philosophical expression." [3] His attitude was largely medieval, and some of his argument is unsatisfactory to a modern reader because of the psychological theory on which it is based. At times, too, he relies not on argument but on analogy. When he attempts to describe how the soul is united to the body, he uses a series of negative similes—the soul in the body is not like a pilot in a ship, nor as a spider in its web, nor as heat in the fire, nor as a voice in the air—followed by a positive simile:

> But as the fair and cheerful morning light
>   Doth here and there her silver beams impart,
> And in an instant doth herself unite
>   To the transparent air, in all and part:
>
> Still resting whole, when blows the air divide,
>   Abiding pure when th'air is most corrupted;
> Throughout the air her beams dispersing wide,
>   And when the air is tossed, not interrupted . . .

Although the argument is dated, the poem remains a masterpiece. It is a very lucid piece of exposition, unequaled by any poet before Dryden; the quatrains are managed with great skill and variety; the diction is singularly pure; and Davies exhibits, as Eliot claims, "great felicity of phrase." [4]

Davies matured early as a poet; and, poetically speak-

[3] *On Poets and Poetry* (1957), p. 135.
[4] *Ibid.*

ing, he died young. There is one poem in which he compares the effect of love on his imagination to the reviving effect of the sun on a butterfly;[5] but the impression left on the reader is more of the sterility than of its cure:

> So my gay Muse which did my heart possess,
>   And in my youthful fantasy doth reign;
> Which cleared my forehead with her cheerfulness
>   And gave a lively warmth unto my brain:
>
> With sadder study, and with grave conceit
>   Which late my imagination entertained,
> Began to shrink and lose her active heat.
>   And dead as in a lethargy remained.

Davies wrote few good lyrics; and this probably accounts for the way he is ignored by the general reader and underrated as a poet.

JOHN DONNE

Although the poems of John Donne (1573–1631) were not published until much later, there is plenty of evidence that many of them were written in the sixteenth century. All the satires and elegies, *The Progress of the Soul,* the epigrams, and about half the songs and sonnets were written before Donne, an ardent playgoer with a reputation for wildness, had reached the age of thirty.

The epigrams were much admired by Donne's contemporaries, and the best of them are wittier and more polished than those of Sir John Davies and Sir John

---

[5] "Like as the divers-freckled butterfly." The poem is not certainly by Davies.

Harrington, but they are nonetheless of minor interest. Donne was writing his satires during the decade when Lodge, Hall, and Marston were writing theirs. Donne's are more rugged than Lodge's or Hall's and more lucid than Marston's. Elizabethans noted that Juvenal was rougher in his versification than Horace; and in writing their invective they seem deliberately to have made their verse harsh. Where Donne scores over his rivals is, first, in that he is much more forceful and colloquial; second, in that he is more amusing and not given merely to name-calling; and third, in that there is much more reality in the persons and things he is satirizing—they are not mere types and abstractions.

Some of the elegies are similar in style to the satires (e.g., "Jealousy," "The Anagram," and "A Tale of a Citizen and His Wife"—if this last one is Donne's); but the best of them are closer in spirit to the songs and sonnets. Jonson declared, in a famous phrase, that Donne was "the best poet in the world for some things"; and such elegies as "Love's Progress," "To His Mistress Going to Bed," and "On His Mistress" are unequaled expressions of sexual passion. The last of these is a plea to his mistress not to accompany him overseas, dressed as a page. It opens with a powerful and passionate conjuration in fairly smooth verse:

> By our first strange and fatal interview,
> By all desires which thereof did ensue,
> By our long starving hopes, by that remorse
> Which my words' masculine persuasive force
> Begot in thee, and by the memory
> Of hurts, which spies and rivals threatened me,
> I calmly beg: but by thy father's wrath,
> **By** all pains which want and divorcement hath,

I conjure thee, and all the oaths which I
And thou have sworn to seal joint constancy,
Here I unswear, and overswear them thus,
Thou shalt not love by ways so dangerous.

In the middle section of the poem, in which Donne imagines the dangers likely to befall a woman in man's apparel, the verse becomes more broken and irregular, nearer to that of the satires. Then at the end, he urges his mistress not to

            bless nor curse
Openly love's force, nor in bed fright thy Nurse
With midnight's startings, crying out "oh, oh
Nurse, oh my love is slain! I saw him go
O'er the White Alps alone; I saw him, I,
Assailed, fight, taken, stabbed, bleed, fall and die."

This, like several of the elegies and many of the songs and sonnets, is a kind of dramatic monologue, and it would be wrong to assume that it is a piece of autobiography.

The songs and sonnets, with their colloquial diction, their realism, their original imagery, their wit, their far-fetched conceits, and their fusion of thought and feeling were written in reaction against the dominant modes of Elizabethan love poetry: its aureate diction, idealism, pastoralism, conventionality, and lack of psychological realism. The better poets, of course, transcended these modes. As Donne in his youth was a frequenter of the theater, it is not surprising that he introduced into his lyrics many of the characteristics of dramatic poetry.

The abrupt openings of several of Donne's best-known poems,

For God's sake, hold your tongue and let me love,

and

> He is stark mad, who ever says
> That he hath been in love an hour,

and

> Busy old fool, unruly sun,

are examples of his dramatic sense. The poems are often dramatic monologues with an audience of one woman. One short example may be quoted in full:

> When by thy scorn, O murdress, I am dead,
>   And that thou think'st thee free
>   From all solicitation from me,
> Then shall my ghost come to thy bed,
>   And thee, feigned vestal, in worse arms shall see;
> Then thy sick taper will begin to wink,
>   And he, whose thou art then, being tired before,
> Will, if thou stir, or pinch to wake him, think
>   Thou call'st for more,
> And in false sleep will from thee shrink;
> And then, poor aspen wretch, neglected thou,
>   Bathed in a cold quicksilver sweat will lie,
>   A verier ghost than I.
>   What I will say, I will not tell thee now,
> Lest that preserve thee; and since my love is spent,
> I'had rather thou should'st painfully repent,
> Than by my threat'nings rest still innocent.

In the theater, toward the end of the last decade of the century, there was a move toward greater psychological realism, in the characterization, in the style of acting, and in the use of more colloquial language; and perhaps these tendencies influenced Donne's poetry. A few years later, in the first decade of the seventeenth century, a number of dramatists began to display some of the characteristics of metaphysical poetry. Donne's poems do not seem to have been widely circulated until somewhat later, when his influence on nondramatic poets became apparent; but a poet who was a keen play-goer would be likely to associate with dramatists.

MINOR POETS

The nondramatic poets who have been discussed above produced a body of work of continuing interest and importance. There were, of course, many others who are of interest only to the specialist. Among these we might include the satirists who have been mentioned above in connection with Donne. A large number of verse satires were published in the last years of the sixteenth century by Joseph Hall, John Marston, Thomas Lodge, William Rankins, Edward Guilpin, and others; but the interest they still possess is social and historical rather than literary. Marston's couplets are rugged, and Hall's and Lodge's comparatively smooth; but even at their best they are lacking in wit:

> Great is the folly of a feeble brain,
> O'er-ruled with love and tyrannous disdain;
> For love, however in the basest breast
> It breeds high thoughts that feed the fancy best,
> Yet is he blind, and leads poor fools awry,
> While they hang gazing on their mistress' eye.
>
> *(Hall)*

> He is a gallant fit to serve my Lord,
> Which claws, and soothes him up, at every word;
> That cries, when his lame poesy he hears,
> "Tis rare, my Lord, 'twill pass the nicest ears."
> This makes Amphidius welcome to good cheer,
> And spend his master forty pounds a year.
>
> *(Lodge)*

More interesting than the satirists are the minor poets who earn a place in the anthologies with their occasional successes. Nicholas Breton, for example, was a voluminous writer whose prose works are often charming and whose verse is competently dull. But now and again he rose above his pedestrian level to write a well-turned lyric, such as the popular "In the merry month of May." Richard Barnfield (1574–1627), to take another example, wrote feeble sonnets; but some of his longer poems and one or two short lyrics are fresh and musical. Robert Southwell (d. 1595), a saintly man who turned out quantities of religious verse, has three or four fine lyrics to his credit, including the famous "Burning Babe."

Lastly, a word should be said about the verse translations of the last years of Elizabeth's reign. Edward Fairfax's version of Tasso's *Godfrey of Bulloigne* (1600) far surpasses Golding's Ovid and Chapman's Homer; and Sir John Harrington's *Orlando Furioso* (1591), though it fails to convey the more poetical qualities of Ariosto's epic, is continuously entertaining.

Suggested Reading

The miscellanies have been edited by H. E. Rollins (Cambridge, Mass.: Harvard Univ. Press, 1924–37).

The songbooks were collected by E. H. Fellowes in *English Madrigal Verse* (Oxford Univ. Press, 1931).

The standard editions of the various poets discussed in this chapter are:

Campion, edited by P. Vivian (Oxford: Clarendon Press, 1909).

Ralegh, edited by A. M. C. Latham (London: Routledge and Kegan Paul, 1951).

Chapman, edited by P. B. Bartlett (New York: P.M.L.A., 1941). Chapman's Homer, edited by Allardyce Nicoll (London: Routledge and Kegan Paul, 1957).

Sir John Davies in *Silver Poets of the Sixteenth Century,* edited by G. Bullett (London: Dent, 1947).

Donne, edited by H. J. C. Grierson (Oxford: Clarendon Press, 1912). Donne's *Songs and Sonnets,* the *Elegies,* and the *Divine Poems* have been edited by Helen Gardner (Oxford: Clarendon Press, 1952, 1965).

Fairfax's translation of Tasso, edited by J. Nelson (New York: Capricorn, 1963) and Harrington's translation of Ariosto, edited G. Hough (Carbondale: Southern Illinois Univ. Press, 1962) are now available.

There is a study of Campion by M. M. Kastendieck (New York: Columbia Univ. Press, 1938); and two of Ralegh: *Sir Walter Ralegh* by Philip Edwards (London: Longmans, 1953) and *The Queen and the Poet* by Walter Oakeshott (London: Faber and Faber, 1960).

VI
Some Prose Writers

At the beginning of Elizabeth's reign the best prose was to be found in translations and in the pamphlets written and published abroad or secretly in England by Catholic recusants.

It was natural that, in translating from foreign master-pieces, Elizabethan writers should retain something of the structure of the original prose and should be prevented from dropping into the invertebrate prose of most of their contemporaries. Among the translations published during the first twenty years of the reign may be mentioned three outstanding ones: Sir Thomas Hoby's lively version of *The Courtier* of Castiglione (1561),

William Adlington's equally racy version of *The Golden Ass* of Apuleius (1566), and Thomas Underdowne's *Æthiopian History* of Heliodorus (1569). These were followed by Plutarch's *Lives,* translated by Sir Thomas North (1579), David Rowland's *Lazarillo de Tormes* (1586), Angel Day's *Daphnis and Chloe* (1587), William Burton's *Clitophon and Leucippe* (1597), versions of Pliny, Livy, and Suetonius, Plutarch's *Moralia* by Philemon Holland, and John Florio's translation of Montaigne's *Essais* (1603).

These twelve representative translations vary in kind. Holland, who was described, on account of his extraordinary industry, as "Translator General," gave his public useful and accurate, but somewhat pedestrian, versions of the classics. On the other hand, Underdowne seems to have had small Latin and less Greek, and he often mistakes the meaning of his original. Yet in vigor, in felicitous choice of words, and in color his style is superior to that of Heliodorus. Day and Adlington combine the virtues of comparative accuracy and sense of style. Florio, it must be confessed, sometimes missed the subtler points in Montaigne's *Essais,* but his colloquial rhythms, his large vocabulary, natural to one who had compiled an English-Italian dictionary, and his homespun phrases make his translation an English classic. It is one of the few books that Shakespeare is known to have possessed. Here, for example, is a passage contrasting man and beast. Montaigne says he often hears people complain

> that man is the only forsaken and outcast creature, naked on the bare earth, fast bound and swathed, having nothing to cover and arm himself withal but the spoil of others;

whereas Nature hath clad and mantled all other creatures, some with shells, some with husks, with rinds, with hair, with wool, with stings, with bristles, with hides, with moss, with feathers, with scales, with fleeces and with silk, according as their quality might need, or their condition require: and hath fenced and armed them with claws, with nails, with talons, with hoofs, with teeth, with stings and with horns, both to assail others and to defend themselves: and hath moreover instructed them in everything fit and requisite for them, as to swim, to run, to creep, to fly, to roar, to bellow and to sing: whereas man only—O silly wretched man!—can neither go, nor speak, nor shift, nor feed himself, unless it be to whine and weep only, except he be taught.

North's Plutarch, the main source of Shakespeare's Roman plays, is another masterpiece. North used Amyot's French version, rather than the original, and the construction and rhythm of his sentences are apt to be loose and careless. The success of his work is in large measure due to the enormous readability of Plutarch's biographies; but not entirely, for North's translation is still more attractive than any later one. His prose is full of vitality and color, as in the description of the first meeting of Antony and Cleopatra. The Greek and Roman heroes do not seem to be remote historical figures: they live and speak almost as Elizabethans. Cato, for example, after stabbing himself with his sword,

fell down upon his bed, and made such a noise with his fall—overthrowing a little table of geometry hard by his bed—that his servants hearing the noise, gave a great shriek for fear.

Or, as another example, the soldier who finds Charmion trimming the dead Cleopatra's diadem

angrily said unto her: "Is that well done, Charmion?"

"Very well," said she again, "and meet for a princess descended from the race of so many noble kings." She said no more, but fell down hard by the bed.

North is at his best in the long set speeches that Plutarch invents for his characters. Volumnia's appeal to Coriolanus, for example, is so effective that Shakespeare was able to follow it closely, as the opening shows:

If we held our peace, my son, and determined not to speak, the state of our poor bodies and present sight of our raiment would easily bewray to thee what life we have led at home since thy exile and abode abroad. But think now with thyself how much more unfortunately than all the women living we are come hither, considering that the sight which should be most pleasant to all other to behold, spiteful fortune hath made most fearful to us: making myself to see my son, and my daughter here, her husband, besieging the walls of his native country. So as that which is the only comfort to all other in their adversity and misery, to pray unto the gods and to call to them for aid is the only thing which plungeth us into most deep perplexity. For we cannot, alas, together pray both for victory for our country and for the safety of thy life also: but a world of grievous curses, yea more than any mortal enemy can heap upon us, are forcibly wrapped up in our prayers.

In addition to translations from the classics and from French, Italian, and Spanish, the period is notable for its rival versions of the Bible. The Geneva version (1560) remained the most popular until the King James version of 1611, and not merely among Puritans. The Bishops' Bible (1568), appointed to be read in churches, was too large in format for domestic use. The Rheims and Douai New Testament (1582) was the one made for use by Catholics. The Bishops' Bible, since it was intended for reading aloud, is rhythmically superior to the others;

but it was not so much a new translation as a revision of previous ones. In the same way the Authorized Version of 1611 owes a great deal to its predecessors, and the translators consulted the Geneva and Catholic versions as well as the Bishops'. It was some years before it displaced the Geneva Bible in popularity, but from the middle of the seventeenth century until the present day its rhythms and phrases have exercised so powerful an influence on generations of people that each new attempt to produce a modern translation has met with complaints: in attempting to be modern, accurate, and lucid, the rhythms and the beauty of diction of the Authorized Version have been destroyed.

We have referred above to the excellence of the prose written by recusants. It has, indeed, been argued by R. W. Chambers[1] and others that native English prose was spoiled at the Renaissance by a concentration on the manner of writing at the expense of the matter. Many textbooks of rhetoric were published, setting forth figures of speech by which the matter could be presented more attractively, or at least more decoratively; and the Elizabethan schoolboy learned the art of writing by imitating Latin prose, especially that of Cicero. It has been argued that, after More, the mainstream of English prose is to be found in the work of the recusants and in the Rheims and Douai Bible and that for a hundred years, through the classical influence of Cicero and Seneca and the influence too of Italian and Spanish literature, the majority of English writers took a wrong turn. Native prose, it is said, resurfaced only with Dryden.

[1] *On the Continuity of English Prose* (Oxford Univ. Press, 1932).

For several reasons, the theory is unsound. First, there were Protestant exiles in the reign of Queen Mary who wrote equally vigorous and plain prose. Second, not every writer of the period put style above matter: Greene, in his later writings, Deloney in his novels, and the travel narratives collected by Hakluyt may be cited as examples. Third, there is something odd about a theory that by implication condemns not merely the Euphuistic and Arcadian styles but the prose of Ralegh and Hooker, Bacon and Donne, Browne, Andrewes, and Jeremy Taylor. It cannot be pretended that any of these writers, with the possible exception of Sir Thomas Browne in some of his works, were too much concerned with decoration and too little concerned with content. Fourth, it should be said that English prose profited from the classical discipline and that a plain or familiar style is not the only kind of excellence.

This is not to deny that some of the recusants write admirably. Many of their pamphlets are colloquial, even slangy, in style, and they are spiced with racy proverbial phrases, witty repartee, and touches of humor. At times they use good-humored raillery and at others biting invective. This is a passage in which Thomas Stapleton attacks Horne:

O M. Horne, your manifold untruths are deciphered and unbuckled, ye are espied, ye are espied, I say, well enough, that ye come not by a thousand yards and more nigh the mark. Your bow is too weak, your arms too feeble, to shoot with any your commendation at this mark: yea, if ye were as good an archer as were that famous Robin Hood or Little John. Well, shift your bow, or at the leastwise your string. Let the Old Testament go, and proceed to your other proofs, wherein we will now see if ye can shoot any straighter.

As an example of graver and more sustained writing, we may take this passage from William Allen's *Apology and True Declaration* (1581), in which he outlines the changes in England between the reigns of Henry VIII and Elizabeth I:

> And it were the pitifullest hazard and uncertainty of our faith and salvation that could be, so to hang on the Prince's will, or the laws (commonly wholly thereon depending) that there could be imagined no nearer way to religion than to believe what our temporal lord and master list. And it is the turpitude of our nation through the whole world, whereat we blush before strangers that sometimes fall into discourse of such things, that in one man's memory and since this strange mutation began, we have had to our Prince a man who abolished the Pope's authority by his laws, and yet in other points kept the faith of his fathers: we have had a child, who by the like laws abolished together with the Papacy the whole ancient religion: we had a woman, who restored both again, and sharply punished Protestants: and lastly her Majesty that now is, who by the like laws hath long since abolished both again, and now severely punisheth Catholics, as the other did Protestants: and all these strange differences within the compass of about thirty years.

"Martin Marprelate" (the pseudonym of a witty Puritan) and the anti-Martinist pamphleteers, who may have included Lyly and Nashe, shared a pretty talent for invective, humor, and a style as colloquial as that of the recusants. Martin himself is more effective than his opponents because, in spite of his fun and scurrility, he was passionately convinced of the rightness of his cause, whereas his opponents took on the task for cash. A specimen of Martin's style may be given from *An Epistle to the Right Puissant and Terrible Priests* (1588):

> Item, may it please your worthy worships to receive this courteously to favour at my hand, without choler or

laughing. For my Lord of Winchester is very choleric and peevish, so are his betters at Lambeth, and Dr. Cousins hath a very good grace in jesting, and I would he had a little more grace, and a handful or two more of learning against he answer the *Abstract* next. Nay, believe me, it is enough for him to answer the *Counterpoison*. And I am none of the malicious sectaries, whereof John of London spake the last Lent, 1588, in his letters written to the Archdeacon of Essex, to forbid public fasts. Ha, ha, Dr. Copcot, are ye there? Why do not you answer the confutation of your sermon at Paul's Cross? It is a shame for your grace John of Canterbury that Cartwright's books have been now a dozen years almost unanswered: you first provoked him to write, and you first have received the foil. If you can answer those books, why do you suffer the Puritans to insult and rejoice at your silence? If you cannot, why are you an Archbishop?

Many of the Puritans deplored the tone of Martin's pamphlets, and obviously this is not the way in which theological controversy should be conducted. But it should be remembered that the more sober writings of the Puritans had provoked little in the way of an answer and that Martin was writing at the risk of his life. Critics of Milton have equally deplored the tone of his later anti-episcopal pamphlets, though he adopted something of the Martinist style only when his graver writings had been met with scurrilous abuse of his character.

It was left to Thomas Hooker to raise the controversy to a higher plane. The first four books of *The Laws of Ecclesiastical Polity,* his great apologia for the Anglican Church, appeared in 1594; Book V was published three years later; and the remaining three were published at intervals half a century and more after Hooker's death. It used to be thought that his drafts of these books were altered to make them conform to later ideas of Church government; but it is probable that the alterations were not serious.

The general tone of Hooker's treatise is one of sweet reasonableness. Whereas Martin Marprelate and his opponents used wit and invective, aiming to ridicule and score points off the other side, Hooker deliberately eschewed "disdainful sharpness of wit." He wrote, as he said, "with charity and meekness." He urges the Puritans to re-examine their case, point by point, and to lay aside their bitterness:

> Think ye are men, deem it not impossible for you to err; sift impartially your own hearts, whether it be of force of reason or vehemency of affection which hath bred and still doth feed these opinions in you.

He objected to the dogmatism of Calvinism, but speaks of Calvin himself with respect. Unlike most of his contemporaries, Hooker thought that heretics would be saved. He did not believe that any system of government was unalterable: he wished each one to be discussed on its merits.

Hooker's style is for the most part simple and unadorned. The subject matter of most of his treatise does not lend itself to sublimity. When, for example, he is arguing in the second and third books that the Scriptures are not the sole guide for human behavior and that they do not lay down rules for the externals of church worship and government, our interest is held by the lucidity of his reasoning. He had an extraordinarily clear and logical mind, and this is reflected in his prose. Although he had a brilliant grasp of essentials, Hooker was a man of deep feeling. He hated the way in which the churches were divided, and he longed for their re-union; and he believed that the beliefs they held in common were more important than those on which they disagreed. In discussing, for example, the question of whether Christ was actually present in the bread and wine of the Eucharist, he declares:

> What these elements are in themselves it skilleth not . . . why should any cogitation possess the mind of a faithful communicant but this: "O my God, Thou art true! O my soul, thou art happy!"

As an example of Hooker's style, we may take this passage in which he is speaking of the advantages of civilization:

> We all make complaint of the iniquity of our times; not unjustly, for the days are evil. But compare them with those times wherein there were no civil societies, with those times wherein there was as yet no manner of public regiment established, with those times wherein there were not above eight righteous persons living upon the face of the earth; and we have surely good cause to think that God hath blessed us exceedingly, and hath made us behold most happy days. To take away all such mutual grievance, injuries and wrongs, there was no way but only by growing upon composition and agreement amongst themselves; by ordaining some kind of government public, and by yielding themselves subject thereunto; that unto whom they granted authority to rule and govern, by them the peace, tranquillity and happy estate of the rest might be procured.

The long, beautifully articulated sentences and the way the sense is guided by the rhythm are far beyond the reach of even the best prose writers of the early part of Elizabeth's reign; and here and there, particularly in Book I, where Hooker is writing of the rule of divinely ordered law, he rises to magnificence. The superbly controlled structure and rhythm of the third sentence of the following passage is clearly the work of a great stylist:

> He made a law for the rain. He gave his decree unto the sea that the waters should not pass his commandment. Now if nature should intermit her course, and leave altogether, though it were but for a while, the observation of her own laws; if those principal and mother elements of the world whereof all things in this lower world are made should lose the qualities which now they have; if the frame of that heavenly arch erected over our heads should loosen and dissolve itself; if celestial spheres should forget their wonted motions and by irregular volubility turn themselves any way as it might happen; if the prince of the lights of heaven, which now as a giant doth run his unwearied course, should as it were, through a languishing faintness, begin to stand and to rest himself; if the moon should wander from her beaten way, the times and seasons of the year blend themselves by disordered and confused mixture, the winds breathe out their last gasp, the clouds yield no rain, the earth be defeated of heavenly influence, the fruits of the earth pine away as children at the withered breasts of their mother, no longer able to yield them relief—what would become of man himself whom these things now do all serve? See we not plainly that obedience of creatures unto the law of nature is the stay of the whole world?

A good idea of the normal level of Elizabethan prose is provided by the travelers' tales collected by Richard Hakluyt in *The Principal Navigations, Voyages, Traffics and Discoveries of the English Nation* (1582–99). The book includes previously printed material, including Ralegh's account of the last fight of *The Revenge* and *The Discovery of Guiana,* but also a great many contributions by scores of different travelers who had no experience of authorship. Many of these have no literary importance: they record the day-to-day incidents of voyages in short sentences without color or variety. But, on the other hand, a large number of the narratives, without pretending to literary artifice, are admirable examples of the plain style: lucid, masculine, direct, and concrete; they succeed in giving to the reader a vivid account of the dangers and vicissitudes of the voyages, and the best of them convey a sense of the excitement and strangeness of the landscapes and customs of newly discovered lands. Some of the accounts, including Ralegh's, were doubtless written as propaganda to persuade people to invest in future voyages and to compete with the profitable Spanish trade. But Hakluyt's collection, inspired by patriotic feeling, is an impressive memorial to the seamen of the Elizabethan period.

The Elizabethans were anxious to learn not merely about the unexplored regions of the world but also about the history of England. Foxe's *Acts and Monuments* (1563)—"The Book of Martyrs" as it is usually called —gave a remarkably full account of the Marian persecution. Stow's *Survey of London* (1598) and the numerous editions of his *Chronicles* that appeared between 1565 and 1618, pedestrian as they are, obviously answered a real need. On a rather higher level, Holinshed's *Chronicles* (1577) provided a history of Britain from the earliest times. Holinshed made little attempt to sift historical fact from legend—Lear and Cymbeline figure in his pages as well as John and Henry VIII— but he was well read in printed sources, and for some reigns he consulted manuscripts. He was more concerned with recording events than with examining historical causes; but, like Livy and Thucydides, he composed appropriate speeches for the more dramatic parts of his narrative. His prose is always workmanlike and sometimes eloquent, as in his account of the meeting of Macduff and Malcolm in England or of Katharine's defense before Henry VIII.

Prose was used for a variety of different purposes. There were textbooks of rhetoric, including Thomas Wilson's *Art of Rhetoric* (1560), which was the first and best, and a later treatise, Abraham Fraunce's *Arcadian Rhetoric* (1588), which takes its examples of rhetorical devices from Sidney's unpublished *Arcadia*; books on education, including *The Schoolmaster* of Roger Ascham (1570), in which the enlightenment and humanity is matched by the quiet persuasiveness of the prose; treatises on witchcraft by the credulous James VI of Scotland, *Demonology* (1597), and by the skeptical Reginald Scot, *The Discovery of Witchcraft* (1584); attacks on the stage, on usurers, and on the manners and morals of the age; treatises on hunting and falconry by George Turberville, the poet; an exposure of a Puritan exorcist by Samuel Harsnet and his *Declaration of Egregious Popish Impostures* (1603), made famous by Shakespeare's use of it in the mad scenes of *King Lear*.

Then there were numerous collections of tales imitated from those of Boccaccio and Cinthio and similar compilations by French writers. These include William Painter's *Palace of Pleasure* (1566), Fenton's *Tragical Discourses* (1567), Whetstone's *Heptameron of Civil Discourses* (1582), and Barnabe Rich's *Farewell to Military Profession* (1581). The full-length works of fiction, beginning with Lyly's *Euphues* (1579), are discussed in Chapter VII; but one writer of fiction may conveniently be mentioned here. Thomas Deloney (d. 1600), the "balleting silk-weaver from Northwich," as Nashe calls him, spent most of his life writing indifferent verse; but toward the end he turned his hand to prose narrative. *The Gentle Craft* served as the source of Dekker's lively comedy, *The Shoemaker's Holiday*; *Jack of Newbury* is the story of a weaver of Henry VIII's reign who married his master's widow and rose to fortune, and it is padded out with romantic anecdotes and economic facts about the industry; *Thomas of Reading,* the third and best of Deloney's narratives, tells of the life and death of a successful merchant.

All three books are episodic, and the stories are eked out with a good deal of irrelevant material; but they all possess a certain gusto, and although Deloney's style is lacking in literary graces it is appropriate to his subject matter. Individual episodes are told with some skill, and in his account of the murder of Thomas of Reading, Deloney's plain style and his restraint enable him to create an astonishingly powerful scene, which is greatly superior to any other passage in his novels. Thomas Cole is about to be murdered by an innkeeper:

> With that Cole beholding his host and hostess earnestly began to start back, saying: "What ail you to look so like pale death? Good Lord, what have you done, that your hands are thus bloody?" "What! my hands?" said his host. "Why, you may see they are neither bloody nor foul. Either your eyes do greatly dazzle, or else fancies of a troubled mind do delude you." "Alas, my host, you may see" (said he) "how weak my wits are; I never had my head so idle before. Come, let me drink once more, and then I will to bed, and trouble you no longer." With that he made himself unready, and his hostess was very diligent to warm a kerchief, and put it about his head. "Good

Lord," said he, "I am not sick, I praise God, but such
an alteration I find in myself as I never did before." With
that the screech-owl cried piteously, and anon after the
night raven sat croaking hard by his window.

The Elizabethan period also saw the publication of
the first English essays. The earliest collection, Haly
Heron's *The Kayes of Connsaile*—the title quibbles on
the name of the dedicatee, John Kay—was published
in the same year as *Euphues,* and like Lyly, Heron was
influenced by the style of George Pettie's *Petite Pallace
of Pettie His Pleasure* (1576). He offers advice on such
subjects as humility, modest behavior, and wine and
women; and his book is intended to be a treatise on how
to behave in society.

Heron is interesting mainly as a pioneer, but with
Francis Bacon's *Essays* (1597) we have an acknowledged
masterpiece, which was enlarged and improved in the
final version, published in 1625. Bacon kept a commonplace book, and each essay is a kind of mosaic of quotations and original aphorisms relating to the topic in
question. The individual sentences are brilliant, and the
essays hold the attention from the opening words, "Men
fear death as children fear to go in the dark." "Revenge
is a kind of wild justice." "He that hath wife and
children hath given hostages to fortune." Such pithy
remarks are not, however, confined to the opening
sentences: "Money is like muck, not good unless it be
spread." "Certainly virtue is like precious odours, most
fragrant when they are incensed or crushed." Many of
Bacon's best sentences are metaphorical, and there is
some excuse for Shelley's claim that Bacon was a poet,
despite the feebleness of his verse.[2] But other poets have

[2] *A Defence of Poetry* (1821).

regarded him with suspicion. Francis Thompson complained that Bacon in the *Essays* made "no attempt at the more complex evolutions of style; and the succession of short barks is apt to get as tiresome as the utterances of a dog." [3] This is hardly a fair criticism: the aphorisms should be savored individually, not gulped at a sitting. Blake's comments, in his copy of the *Essays,* are more penetrating. He regarded Bacon's worldly wisdom as "good advice for Satan's kingdom." The essays are shrewd, politic, realistic pieces of advice on how to get on in the world. In writing of love Bacon can say only that "it doth much mischief," which is true but chilling; and although on friendship he remarks that "faces are but a gallery of pictures, and talk but a tinkling cymbal, where there is no love," he is mainly concerned with the advantages of a friend: to receive one's confidences and to give advice and help. It is a mystery that many people have been able to believe that the author of the *Essays* also wrote Shakespeare's sonnets.

But the tone of the essays is largely determined by the restricted nature of Bacon's purpose; and the aphoristic style is deliberately adopted for the same purpose. This can be seen from the difference of style employed by Bacon in *The Advancement of Learning* (1605), where he had a subject that engaged his deeper feelings. Philosophy and science were able to move him more than personal relations. The prose of this book has a grandeur and amplitude appropriate to the subject:

But the images of men's wits and knowledges remain in books, exempted from the wrong of time, and capable of perpetual renovation. Neither are they fitly to be called

[3] *Works* (1913), III, p. 192.

images, because they generate still, and cast their seeds in
the minds of others, provoking and causing infinite actions and opinions in succeeding ages. So that if the ship
was thought so noble, which carrieth riches and com-
modities from place to place, and consociateth the most
remote regions in participation of their fruits: how much
more are letters to be magnified, which as ships pass
through the vast seas of time, and make ages so distant
to participate of the wisdom, illuminations, and inventions the one of the other?

It can be seen from this passage that Bacon did not
confine himself in the *Essays* to the short aphorism for
lack of ability to write long periodic sentences.

As we have seen, Elizabethans were taught at school
to take Latin prose as their model for writing English.
Cicero was held in the highest esteem, and his modern
disciples classified his rhythms and made collections of
his phrases for use in their own Latin prose; Latin was
still the international language, and Bacon used it in his
major works. Cicero was a suitable model for some kinds
of writing, and some Elizabethans learned a good deal
about the structure of the long periodic sentence from a
study of his work. G. Williamson in *The Senecan Amble*
has shown how the more colloquial style of Seneca
gradually superseded Cicero's as the favorite model while
the highly mannered euphuistic style has been traced
back, through modern imitations in various languages,
to that of Isocrates.

Bacon complained of writers who pursued a style at
the expense of matter; and Senecans as well as Ciceronians were guilty of this fault. But the most guilty were
Lyly and his followers; and euphuism, though its in-
direct influence on dramatic dialogue may have been
salutary, was in itself a stylistic aberration. Some critics,

indeed, regard the Arcadian style as equally deplorable, but it could never be said that Sidney was unconcerned with content.

Although Elizabethan prose matured later than verse, the work of Sidney, Ralegh, Hooker, and Bacon is worthy to stand beside the great poetry of the last decade of Elizabeth's reign. Below these, but still of permanent interest, are a host of varied prose writers: North and Florio, Nashe and Dekker, Greene and Riche, Martin Marprelate, and many writers of pamphlets and sermons. Despite their great variety, they had a number of virtues in common. They had the advantage of writing at a time when the language was rapidly changing and, in particular, when coining words was in vogue, even though controversialists invariably objected to the coinages of their opponents. Closely connected with this freedom was the avoidance by the better writers of stereotyped phrases. Their prose is fresh and vigorous, often colloquial and even earthy; it never gives the impression of having been turned out by a computer. It makes use of vivid metaphor, and it is, finally, admirably concrete. It was not yet an ideal instrument for philosophical discussion, but it was admirably fitted to carry out most of the other functions of prose. By the end of the sixteenth century it could encompass both narrative and description, sublimity and wit, dramatic speech and theological discussion.

Suggested Reading

Elizabethan Prose, edited by Michael Roberts (London: Faber and Faber, 1933), *The Pelican Book of Prose,* Vol. I, edited by Kenneth Muir (Harmondsworth: Penguin Books, 1956), and *Elizabethan Recusant Prose,* edited by A. C. Southern (London: Sands, 1950) are three representative anthologies.

Recommended studies are *The Senecan Amble* by G. Williamson (Univ. of Chicago Press, 1951), which deals with the struggle between the Ciceronians and the Senecans, and *Wit and Rhetoric in the Renaissance* by W. G. Crane (Magnolia, Mass.: Smith, Peter, 1937).

VII
The Dramatists

Until the last two decades of Elizabeth's reign no drama of permanent value seems to have been written. The better plays, *Gorboduc* and Gascoigne's *Supposes,* had been performed by amateurs. The professional companies, who toured the provinces and performed in the innyards of London and later in the theaters that began to be erected, had to make do with very crude plays, if we may judge by those that have survived. The first real theater, which retained some of the characteristics of the innyard and the bear-baiting ring—a platform, a balcony, an unroofed auditorium—was erected in 1576. But there was still a dearth of tolerable drama. Sidney's satirical account of a typical play of the period was not greatly exaggerated:

> You shall have Asia of the one side and Affrick of the other, and so many other under-kingdoms, that the player, when he cometh in, must ever begin with telling where he is, or else the tale will not be conceived. Now ye shall have three ladies walk to gather flowers, and then we must believe the stage to be a garden. By and by we hear news of shipwreck in the same place, and then we are to blame if we accept it not for a rock. Upon the back of that comes out a hideous monster, with fire and smoke, and then the miserable beholders are bound to take it for a cave. While in the meantime two armies fly in, represented with four swords and bucklers, and then what hard heart will not receive it for a pitched field . . . Ordinary it is that two young princes fall in love. After many traverses she is got with child, delivered of a fair boy; he is lost, groweth a man, falls in love, and is ready to get another child; and all this in two hours space.

Sidney was mainly concerned with the failure of the playwrights to obey the unities. Much more serious was the mingling of melodrama and farce, the feeble characterization, and the doggerel verse in which the plays were written.

The situation was entirely transformed between 1580 and 1590 by a group of men with some literary talent, who turned their hands to all kinds of writing: fiction, verse, pamphlets, and plays. They are known as the University Wits, though one of them, Thomas Kyd, never attended a university. But they were all educated men who turned to the stage as a means of earning a living; and they were not, like Shakespeare and Jonson, actors by profession. It was a tragic generation: Robert Greene, after a dissolute life, was carried off by a fever;

Christopher Marlowe was killed, in the last of several brawls in which he engaged, when he was not yet thirty; Thomas Nashe (1567–1601) died young; John Lyly (1554–1606) lived on into the next century, disappointed of his hopes of advancement at court; George Peele (1558–97) it is thought, died of the pox; and only Thomas Lodge (1558–1625), abandoning the stage, lived to be a respectable physician and the translator of Seneca's prose works.

John Lyly began his career in 1578 with a courtesy book masquerading as a novel, *Euphues,* and the style known as euphuism became the fashion and, like most fashions, the object of parody. The style, with its antithetical clauses, its ubiquitous alliteration, and its similes from dubious natural history, was imitated by dozens of writers; and nearly twenty years later Shakespeare parodied it in *1 Henry IV*.

Lyly was drawn to the stage by his employment by the Earl of Oxford, himself a dramatist, by his job in directing the Children of St. Paul's, and perhaps by his hope, which was never realized, of becoming the Master of the Revels. When an edition of his plays was published after his death, they were properly entitled *Court Comedies,* for they were all written with a court audience in mind, and several of them allegorize events at court in a way that would have baffled an audience in a public theater. As the plays were all performed by boys, their success depended not on the acting so much as on the satisfactory delivery of the elegant and witty prose dialogue and on the singing of the charming songs that are interspersed, though it is not certain that the songs printed in 1632 were the ones Lyly had written.

Lyly avoided scenes that might be beyond the powers
of his actors. In his first comedy, for example, Apelles'
declaration of love to Campaspe takes place off stage.
Lyly's audience could be relied upon to appreciate the
wit of the dialogue, to pick up allusions to classical
mythology, and to solve the riddle of his allegories. They
would know that Cynthia in *Endimion,* Sapho in *Sapho
and Phao,* and Diana in *Gallathea* were all representa-
tions of Queen Elizabeth and that Midas, in the play of
that name, written soon after the defeat of the Spanish
Armada, represented Philip of Spain.

Even the earliest plays have witty exchanges between
mischievous pages and amusing farcical scenes. But they
are filled with long euphuistic speeches; the serious characters all talk in the same style; and there is hardly any
action. But if one reads the plays in chronological order,
one notices that Lyly's sense of the dramatic—or of what
he could expect from his actors—gradually increased,
and he learned to vary his prose rhythms. *Campaspe* is
entirely euphuistic. In *Endimion* there are speeches with
so charming a cadence that Lyly has been compared, not
altogether absurdly, with Congreve:

> Believe me, Eumenides, desire dies in the same moment
> that beauty sickens, and beauty fadeth in the same instant
> that it flourisheth. When adversities flow, then love ebbs;
> but friendship standeth stiffly in storms. Time draweth
> wrinkles in a fair face, but addeth fresh colours to a
> fast friend, which neither heat, nor cold, nor misery, nor
> place, nor destiny, can alter or diminish.

Ralph, the clown in *Gallathea,* is more successful than
several of Shakespeare's early clowns, and his speeches
are continuously amusing:

> Of all deaths I would not be drowned, one's clothes will
> be so wet when one is taken up . . . It were a shame a
> little cold water should kill a man of reason, when you
> shall see a poor minnow lie in it, that hath no under-
> standing.

In this play Gallathea and Phillida are disguised as boys
lest they should be sacrificed to a sea monster, and their
scenes together are filled with ingeniously ambiguous
dialogue.

Lyly's most effective play, performed as late as 1589,
was *Mother Bombie*. It has a complex and swiftly
moving plot; there is more wit in the dialogue than in
the previous plays; and, what is more important, the
style is more colloquial and is varied to suit the different characters. The low intelligence of the beautiful but
half-witted Silena, for example, is suggested by the very
rhythms she employs:

> My name is Silena, I care not who know it, so I do not.
> My father keeps me close, so he does; and now I have
> stolen out, so I have, to go to old Mother Bombie, to
> know my fortune, so I will; for I have as fair a face as
> ever trod on shoe sole, and as free a foot as ever looked
> with two eyes.

The play is a model of structure in its symmetrical
grouping of characters, in its clever interweaving of the
various plots, and in its use of the Terentian five-act
structure. It is the best comedy written in English before Shakespeare.

Shakespeare's debt to Lyly was obvious and profound.
In his sense of dramatic structure, in his use of song, in
his interweaving of plots, in his witty servants, Shakespeare found Lyly a fruitful model. Above all, without

the tight structure of Lyly's prose, Shakespeare might have taken much longer to perfect his own comic dialogue.

Another of the University Wits, George Peele, is difficult to assess because only one of his plays, *The Arraignment of Paris,* has come down to us in a satisfactory text. This is a charming pastoral play, partly in rhymed and partly in blank verse, written for performance before the Queen. It is the work of a genuine poet, but one without much sense of the stage. Another pastoral play, *The Hunting of Cupid,* exists only in tantalizingly beautiful extracts. Peele wrote a number of poems, including one of the most beautiful lyrics of the period, "His golden locks time hath to silver turned." After the time of Shakespeare's early histories, Peele wrote *Edward I,* which is dramatically feeble; but his best plays are *The Old Wives' Tale,* which exists only in a truncated text but contains some exquisite songs and a remarkable blend of magic and folklore, and *David and Bethsabe,* which has the loveliest opening of any Elizabethan play but falls off in the later acts.

Christopher Marlowe (1564–93) graduated from Cambridge, decided not to take Holy Orders, and, after some experience as a spy, began to write plays. *1 Tamburlaine,* performed in 1587, in which, as he claimed, he led his audience "From jigging veins of rhyming mother wits," is notable as the first play in which blank verse was used with complete mastery. The blank verse of *Gorboduc* had been wooden, monotonous, and end-stopped. Marlowe, while still taking the line as a unit, contrived to write eloquent, varied, and dramatic verse. It was a discovery that made possible the later achievements of Eliza-

bethan and Jacobean drama; for, whatever the weaknesses of the minor dramatists writing between 1587 and
1640, they nearly all were able to write tolerable blank
verse. It was a medium that avoided the artificiality of
rhymed verse, while retaining where needed the twin
advantages of the poetic and the colloquial.

1 Tamburlaine was followed by a second part a few
months later; and in the few remaining years left to him
Marlowe wrote *The Jew of Malta, Edward II, The
Massacre at Paris, Dido, Queen of Carthage,* and *Doctor
Faustus.* His nondramatic work included a translation,
inaccurate but lively, of Ovid's *Elegies* and an unfinished
poem, *Hero and Leander,* which is his masterpiece. Although, like Shakespeare's *Venus and Adonis,* Marlowe's
poem would have ended tragically, its effect is mainly
one of high comedy; and this is obtained by the frequent
use of hyperbole, by the poet's sly asides, by the use of
feminine rhymes, and by the humorous realism with
which he treats the stories of classical mythology. Marlowe's wit and irony serve the purpose of refining the
poem's sensuality. It is, in Milton's meaning of the
three adjectives, "simple, sensuous and passionate." It
was an extraordinary feat to write a poem that is sensuous in the highest degree, and yet both humorous and
witty; that engages our sympathy for the lovers, even
while we smile at their naïveté; that satisfies us by its
maturity at the same time that it charms us by its
youth.

None of Marlowe's plays is as perfect as this narrative
poem; and this is not merely because two or three of
them have come down to us in corrupt texts. The two
parts of *Tamburlaine,* containing some splendid dramatic

poetry, are unsatisfactory wholes. The only character in whom Marlowe is interested is his hero, who is drawn larger than life. Zenocrate, whom he marries, is little more than an occasion for his splendid speeches. The enemies he overcomes in the course of the two plays are pasteboard figures. The plot is rudimentary. The super-human hero conquers half the world, becoming crueller and more vainglorious with each new conquest. Zeno-crate, who evokes in him the only emotions not purely egotistical, dies; and in the last act Tamburlaine dies too. The man who boasted that he controlled the wheel of fortune is himself brought low. We are presumably meant to think that Tamburlaine is destroyed by his in-ordinate love of power and by his threats against God; but his death is not causally related to what has gone before. The character is a curious mixture: incidents of violence, hideous cruelty, and monomaniacal ambition are interspersed with lyrical eulogies of beauty, which presumably express the feelings of the poet.

The Jew of Malta is much more successful as a play. Critics used to argue that the latter part of the play was crude melodrama, which blended awkwardly with the great poetry of the opening scene. More recently T. S. Eliot and others have described the play as a farce;[1] and the 1965 production at Stratford, which underlined the play's sardonic humor, showed that there was no falling off in the later acts. Barabas' opening speech, expressing his love of wealth, is a necessary prologue to what follows. For the loss of his wealth turns the Jew into a homicidal maniac whose revenges eventually recoil on

[1] T. S. Eliot, *Selected Essays* (New York: Harcourt, Brace & World, 1932), p. 123.

his own head. But Marlowe uses his plot to satirize the Machiavellian policy of the Christians, as he had done in the Orcanes scenes in *Tamburlaine,* so that we are left rejoicing in the way Barabas is hoist with his own petard, but also smiling wryly at the pious sentiments with which the play concludes:

> let due praise be given,
> Neither to Fate, nor Fortune, but to Heaven.

The Jew of Malta has fewer detachable passages of good poetry than *Tamburlaine*; but the plot is managed with greater skill, and the characterization is much more successful.

Doctor Faustus contains allusions to events that took place after Marlowe's death; and though, by the bibliographical skill of Sir Walter Greg, something like the original play has been reconstructed, it was probably written in collaboration. Most critics have deplored the unevenness of the play. The opening scenes, the appearance of Helen, and the final scene are so magnificent that the scenes of clowning and conjuring seem out of keeping. But it has been urged by recent critics that the farcical scenes are schematically related to the tragic scenes; that the feeble use to which Faustus puts his supernatural powers, instead of toward the attainment of universal knowledge, is an intentional irony; and that an Elizabethan audience would have no difficulty in accepting the violent changes of tone. However that may be, there are signs that some of Marlowe's original verse has been turned into prose; and some of the existing verse could not have been written by Marlowe at any period of his career.

The inordinate desires of Marlowe's main tragic heroes

include conquest (Tamburlaine), wealth (Barabas), power (Guise in *The Massacre at Paris*), homosexual love (Edward II), and knowledge (Faustus). We may suppose that the story of a scholar, Faustus, who sells his soul to the devil for universal knowledge, was the closest to Marlowe's personal interests, especially as he was trained in theology. But of his atheistical and heretical views, of which he was accused at the time of his death, there is no trace in the play. It is, indeed, so orthodox that it has been called the last of the morality plays.

Some critics, influenced by their knowledge of Marlowe's table talk, have argued that the poet identified himself with his hero, who, they claimed, symbolized Renaissance man breaking free from the restrictive dogmas and superstitions imposed by the church; and that Helen of Troy is a symbol of "the indestructible beauty of Greek Art." But the play itself gives no warrant for this interpretation. It is clear from the start that Faustus is tempted by the fame and power that knowledge brings; that he rejects theology out of pride; that when he has a chance of questioning Mephistophilis he wants to avoid knowledge of God and damnation; and that he puts his supernatural power to childish uses. What is still more significant is that when he takes Helen for his paramour it is to try to stifle thoughts of his approaching end: that a devil has assumed the "pleasing shape" of Helen and that to have sexual intercourse with a devil was thought to be a sin for which there was no forgiveness. If we decline to accept the fact that Faustus sinned and regard his recourse to the black art as a laudable attempt to widen the bounds of human knowledge, the play becomes nonsense.

The nature of the play does not require any great

subtlety of characterization; but the two main characters are well drawn. The soliloquies of Faustus and the
appearance of the good and evil angels bring out the
conflict in his soul; and the melancholy of Mephistophilis
at "being deprived of everlasting bliss" makes him more
than a stage devil.

The opening soliloquy, the signing of the bond, and
the vision of Helen are all impressive; but Marlowe rises
to his greatest heights in the prose scene with the
scholars, just before the end, and in the final soliloquy.[2]
The prose scene is not, as some have thought, to relieve
the tension, for it arouses pity and terror more effectively than most of the verse scenes. It is rather to re-
mind us of what Faustus might have been, to show by
the affection of his friends that he is a "branch that
might have grown full straight" and, by his anxiety for
the safety of his friends, that he is not wholly evil. The
prose is magnificently rhythmed and would alone prove
that Marlowe was a great dramatist:

> But Faustus' offence can ne'er be pardoned. The Serpent
> that tempted Eve may be saved, but not Faustus. Ah,
> Gentlemen! hear me with patience, and tremble not at
> my speeches. Though my heart pants and quivers to re-
> member that I have been a student here these thirty years,
> O would I had never seen Wertenberge, never read book.
> And what wonders I have done, all Germany can witness,

[2] In between these scenes Marlowe's collaborator has inserted a
kind of peep show of the tortures of hell and the joys of heaven,
which is a vulgar letdown after Mephistophilis has told us that
hell is the deprivation of God:
Hell hath no limits, nor is circumscribed
In one self place; but where we are is hell,
And where hell is there must we ever be.

yea, all the world—for which Faustus hath lost both
Germany and the world, yea, heaven itself, heaven, the
seat of God, the throne of the blessed, the kingdom of
joy, and must remain in hell for ever.

But the final soliloquy is even greater. It conveys with
tremendous force the agony of the hero's last hour: its
swift changes of mood, his inability to repent, and, above
all, his terror of everlasting damnation. In so doing,
Marlowe made as great a revolution in the writing of
blank verse as he had done earlier with the more regular
verse of *Tamburlaine*. If one compares one of the best
passages in *1 Tamburlaine* with the opening of Faustus'
soliloquy, one is impressed by the distance Marlowe had
traveled in the space of five years:

Nature that framed us of four elements,
Warring within our breasts for regiment,
Doth teach us all to have aspiring minds.
Our souls, whose faculties can comprehend
The wondrous architecture of the world,
And measure every wandering planet's course,
Still climbing after knowledge infinite,
And always moving as the restless spheres,
Wills us to wear ourselves and never rest,
Until we reach the ripest fruit of all,
That perfect bliss and sole felicity
The sweet fruition of an earthly crown.
. . .
Ah, Faustus!
Now hast thou but one bare hour to live,
And then thou must be damned perpetually.
Stand still, you ever-moving spheres of heaven,
That time may cease, and midnight never come.
Fair Nature's eye, rise, rise again, and make
Perpetual day; or let this hour be but
A year, a month, a week, a natural day,
That Faustus may repent and save his soul.

The irregularities in the verse—the juxtaposition of stressed syllables and the violent enjambment—which express the urgency and terror of the situation, were as audacious as they were unique.

The evidence suggests that *Doctor Faustus* came at the end of Marlowe's career. Another late play, *The Massacre at Paris,* exists only in a truncated and corrupt form. But enough remains of it to show that Guise, a follower of Machiavelli's supposed principles, must have been one of Marlowe's best-drawn characters. *Dido, Queen of Carthage,* ascribed on the title page to Marlowe and Nashe, though every scene bears the impress of Marlowe's hand, may have been written before he left Cambridge and revised later. Based on Virgil's account in the *Æneid,* it is notable for the description of the fall of Troy and for the fact that it contains Marlowe's only full-length portrait of a woman. It has been somewhat undervalued, partly because of its supposed early date and partly because it contains little of the characteristic Marlovian splendor.

The remaining play, *Edward II,* had the advantage of being written after *Henry VI.* But Marlowe, though he learned from his great rival, went beyond him in creating a dramatic unity out of the facts of history. He had learned by this time the necessity of taking pains with his subsidiary characters and of avoiding long declamatory speeches. Five or six of his characters are well drawn, and there is plenty of give-and-take in the dialogue. The only serious weakness is in the portrait of the Queen, whose transformation from a loving wife to the mistress of her husband's murderer has to be taken on trust.

There is no suggestion in Marlowe's play—as there

was to be in *Richard II*—of the divine right of kings. But Marlowe gives us an impressive picture of the way Edward is destroyed by his love of favorites, and he conveys the pathos of his fall and the horror of his murder in unforgettable scenes. All readers have admired Edward's account of his treatment in the dungeon and Mortimer's farewell as he goes out to execution:

> Farewell, fair Queen: weep not for Mortimer,
> That scorns the world, and as a traveller
> Goes to discover countries yet unknown.

Less often noticed is the way Gaveston's original motives are entirely selfish; but in the end he has a genuine affection for the King. And, in the same way, the cold-blooded careerists, Baldock and Spenser, are converted not merely to love of the King but to pious resignation.

Shakespeare developed his own dramatic verse from Marlowe's; he learned from him something of dramatic structure; and his conception of the tragic hero seems to have developed from Marlowe's. It is hardly too much to say that if Shakespeare had fallen in a tavern brawl, as Marlowe did, at the age of twenty-nine, we should have regarded Marlowe as the greater dramatist, even though he had written no comedies to compare with Shakespeare's.

Robert Greene, six years older than Marlowe, was attracted to the stage by the resounding success of *Tamburlaine*. Before then he had written mainly novels. He began as an avowed imitator of *Euphues*. *Mamillia* (1580) has the same theme of infidelity, but in this and in most of his other writings Greene makes his men inconstant and his women extravagantly virtuous and forgiving. Four years and several books later Greene was still writing in the euphuistic style; but in *Gwydonius: The Carde of Fancie* he has, for the first time, a reasonably interesting story, spoiled only by the overhearing of a soliloquy. *Arbasto,* written in the same year, has a preposterous plot. The hero marries a woman who finds a love letter previously written to her sister. She dies of a broken heart. The sister then falls in love with him and, on being repulsed, also dies of a broken heart. By the time he wrote *Pandosto,* the source of *The Winter's Tale,* in 1588, Greene had purged his style of its excessive euphuism, perhaps under the influence of Angel Day's delightful translation of *Daphnis and Chloe.* But although the novel is well written, it suffers from a tedious complication, when Pandosto falls in love with his own daughter. His best novel, however, was *Menaphon,* published in 1589, which has a complicated plot, fine descriptions, and some charming songs interspersed. The prose is lucid and elegant, probably owing something to Sidney's *Arcadia,* which was circulating in manuscript. In the convention in which Greene was writing, derived ultimately from Greek romances, fantastic incidents and extraordinary coincidences abound; disguise is impenetrable; heroines are ageless; and the characters are all stock types. But the novel is redeemed by the grace of the prose and the charm of the pastoral atmosphere.

There followed a series of novels concerned with the repentance of prodigals, *Never Too Late, Francesco's Fortunes,* and others, which contain an element of autobiography. In the avowed autobiographical works, *The Groatsworth of Wit* and *The Repentance of Robert Greene,* there is probably an element of fiction. In these last two works, and in the lively series of coney-catching[3] pamphlets that purported to expose the tricks of the criminal underworld, Greene's style is to be seen at its best: simple, direct, and unaffected. In the *Repentance,* for example, he gives us his reply to his friends' warning that he was heading straight for hell:

> Hell (quoth I) what talk you of hell to me? I know if I once come there, I shall have the company of better men than myself. I shall also meet with some mad knaves in that place, and so long as I shall not sit there alone, my care is the less. But you are mad folks (quoth I) for if I feared the judges of the bench no more than I dread the judgements of God, I would before I slept dive into one carle's bags or other and make merry with the shells I found in them so long as they would last.

By this time Greene was on his deathbed. After *Menaphon,* and before the last series of pamphlets, he had written a number of plays. *Alphonsus* is a bad imitation of *Tamburlaine; Orlando Furioso,* taken from Ariosto's poem, is not much better, though it contains some tolerable imitations of Marlovian blank verse; *A Looking-Glass for London and England* (written in collaboration with Thomas Lodge) is based on the story of Jonah, the sins of Nineveh being a reflection of the sins of London. Greene's only successful plays were his last, *Friar Bacon and Friar Bungay* and *James IV.* Both plays are well constructed. Lyly's underplots are not usually organically related to the main plot, but Greene's are linked with some skill. He was renowned as a "plotter" (i.e., a writer of scenarios), and we can see

[3] Coney-catchers were confidence tricksters.

that he deserved his reputation in this respect. One main plot of *Friar Bacon and Friar Bungay* is concerned with Bacon's project to surround England with a wall of brass, which is frustrated by the thick-wittedness of Miles, the clown. Linked with this is Bacon's defeat of the foreign magician, Vandermast. The other main plot is concerned with the rivalry of the Prince and Lacy for the love of Margaret, a country girl; and this is related to the magic plot when the Prince sees in Bacon's glass the treachery of his friend. Magic is likewise used in the scene where Lambert and Serlsby kill each other, watched by their sons in Bacon's glass. The sons, too, fight and are slain; and this leads Bacon to forswear necromancy.

But in spite of the variety and ingenuity of the play, it remains something of a disappointment. The verse is mostly pedestrian though it contains some fine passages and some Skeltonic doggerel. What is more serious is the weakness of the characterization, although many critics have singled this out for special praise. Margaret has been described as "English and lifelike as well as idealised and charming" [4] and compared absurdly with Shakespeare's heroines. In fact Margaret's character is largely determined by the plot, and some of the sentiments put into her mouth do not suggest the simple country girl she is supposed to be. When, to try her constancy, Lacy pretends he is going to marry another, she decides to become a nun, but when she learns the truth, she breaks her vow and marries him. The character is so unreal that she does not even think that Lacy has done anything wrong.

[4] A. Thorndike, *Minor Elizabethan Drama* (London: Dent, 1910), p. xii.

Dorothea, in *James IV,* has been praised even more rapturously. She would, we are told, "do honour to Shakespeare." [5] Like Imogen, she forgives the husband who has tried to murder her; and like many of Shakespeare's heroines she disguises herself as a boy. But there the resemblance ends. For Posthumus has reason to believe that Imogen is guilty of adultery, and he repents of his jealous fury before he knows she is innocent. James IV orders the murder of his wife without any such excuse; and Dorothea behaves all the time like a patient Griselda, telling her would-be murderer at the end of the play, "Tut, but a little fault." The King's conduct is so atrocious that Dorothea's continuing love for him is incredible. Greene overdoes the Elizabethan convention by which characters inform the audience of their nobility and virtue so that Dorothea, like Margaret, is a mere puppet. A minor character, Lady Anderson, who falls in love with the disguised Dorothea, is depicted more successfully; but the characterization is the main weakness of *James IV*. Once again Greene's plotting is greatly superior to his execution.

Although *James IV* purports to be an historical play, it is based on a tale by Cinthio, and Greene deserves the credit for being the first to adapt an Italian novel for the English stage. Shakespeare was well acquainted with Greene's works: he made use of the coney-catching pamphlets as well as *Pandosto* for *The Winter's Tale*; from another book he picked up a few hints for *Troilus and Cressida*; and he may have learned something of the art of plotting from a study of Greene's later plays.

[5] J. C. Collins in his edition of the play.

But the forgiveness exercised by Imogen and Hermione owes nothing to the Griselda-like Dorothea.

Thomas Lodge was almost as prolific as Greene, and his work was even more varied in kind. Between 1579 and 1596 he wrote the earliest example of a narrative poem based on Ovid, *Scillaes Metamorphosis,* in the same six-line stanza that Shakespeare was to use in *Venus and Adonis*; *A Fig for Momus,* the first Elizabethan verse satire, written in more polished couplets than those employed by Marston in *The Scourge of Villainie* and more vigorous than those of Joseph Hall in *Virgidemiarum,* whose "toothless satires" (as the author called them) Milton was to ridicule more than forty years later; a *Defence of Stage Plays,* written, like Sidney's *Defence* in reply to Gosson; several satirical works in prose; a feeble sonnet sequence, *Phillis,* in which he tried to emulate Sidney; four novels, of which the best are *Rosalynde* and *A Margarite of America*; a play written, as we have seen, in collaboration with Robert Greene and partly based on his own pamphlet, *An Alarum Against Usurers*; and *The Wounds of Civil War,* the first Elizabethan play on Roman history.

Lodge was a writer of considerable breadth, and in several fields a pioneer. He was an indifferent poet, except in the songs scattered through his novels; a respectable satirist, though lacking in wit; and a workmanlike, but unexciting, dramatist. His best work, apart from his later translations, is to be found in his novels. *Rosalynde,* well known as the source of *As You Like It,* deserves to be read for its own sake. It is a charmingly written pastoral tale, slow-moving, with long artificial speeches, but maintaining its interest by the variety of its incidents and by the interspersed eclogues and songs. One of the best songs begins:

Love in my bosom like a bee
  Doth suck his sweet.
Now with his wings he plays with me,
  Now with his feet.
Within mine eyes he makes his nest,
His bed amidst my tender breast;
My kisses are his daily feast;
And yet he robs me of my rest.
  Ah wanton, will ye?

And if I sleep, then percheth he
  With pretty flight,
And makes his pillow of my knee
  The livelong night.
Strike I my lute, he tunes the string;
He music plays if so I sing;
He lends me every lovely thing;
Yet cruel he my heart doth sting.
  Whist, wanton, still ye!

Thomas Nashe was mainly a pamphleteer. His only surviving play, *Summer's Last Will and Testament,* was written for a private performance, and it is more like a masque than an ordinary play. But it contains some excellent verse and some of the loveliest songs of the period. His elegy on Marlowe, extant in the eighteenth century, has disappeared; and his one surviving non-dramatic poem is mildly obscene.

His prose work is of various kinds. His *Anatomy of Absurditie* (1589) and *Pierce Penniless* (1592) are satirical; *Christ's Tears Over Jerusalem* (1593) is an attack on the sins of Londoners; *The Unfortunate Traveller* (1594) is the first English picaresque novel; and *The Terrors of the Night* (1594) is mostly taken up with a strange tale of a haunting, which is thought to be aimed at Chapman. *Nashe's Lenten Stuffe* (1599), written at Lowestoft in praise of red herring, is chiefly notable for a prose parody of *Hero and Leander*. Nashe had earlier become involved in the Martin Marprelate controversy, in which, as we have seen, a witty nonconformist had written a series of pamphlets attacking episcopacy: Nashe wrote on the side of the bishops. He also engaged in a pamphlet war with a Cambridge don, Gabriel Harvey, who had attacked Greene after his death. Nashe sprang to the defense of his friend and wrote a series of pamphlets full of boisterous invective and amusing ridicule —but they go on too long.

Nashe is at his best when he is not trying to be serious. The denunciation of sin in *Christ's Tears,* eloquent as it is, appears to be that of a natural jester putting on an act as Jeremiah. Even the horrific incident near the end of *The Unfortunate Traveller,* where the villain is killed while he is blaspheming so that he will be damned, is overwritten; Cutwolf replies to Esdras' appeals for mercy:

> Though I knew God would never have mercy on me, except I have mercy on thee, yet of thee no mercy would I have . . . I tell thee, I would not have undertook so much toil to gain heaven as I have done in pursuing thee for revenge: . . . Look how my feet are blistered with following thee from place to place. I have riven my throat with overstraining it to curse thee. I have ground my teeth to powder with grating and grinding them together for anger when any hath named thee . . . My eyes have broken their strings with staring and looking ghastly as I stood devising how to frame or set my countenance when I met thee.

It is unlikely that Nashe intended this to be comic.

None of Nashe's works is a unified work of art. *The*

Unfortunate Traveller consists of a series of brilliant episodes, satirical, gruesome, fantastic, realistic, even sadistic, by turns. It is continuously interesting, but in the end it leaves us with no clear impression except of extraordinary vitality, and this is given mainly by the vigor and inventiveness of Nashe's style. This is seen at its best in the first part of *Pierce Penniless,* where the hero, who is clearly Nashe's persona, makes his supplication to the devil, whose servant he meets in St. Paul's, "a neat, pedantical fellow in form of a citizen." The complaints of the seven deadly sins are lively and witty; but Nashe padded out his pamphlet with an obscure allegorical tale and extracts from Georgius Pictorius' treatise on demonology.

The same combination of brilliant parts and imperfect wholes is to be found in all Nashe's works. Three or four of the songs in *Summer's Last Will and Testament* are jewels in a comparatively dull setting. The story of Hero and Leander and the tale of the Pope and the Herring in *Nashe's Lenten Stuffe* are much more interesting than the rest of the pamphlet. But even the worst of Nashe's writings contain intermittent flashes of wit and humor; and the quirks of his colloquial speech, the raciness of his vocabulary, and the vigor of his mockery and invective can still delight.

Nashe had few imitators, his prose being the reflection of a unique and eccentric mind. Thomas Dekker in *The Wonderful Year* (1603), the year of the Queen's death and of a visitation of the plague, seems to base his style on *Christ's Tears*; but, if so, he wrote with greater restraint and without the straining after sublimity that mars Nashe's serious work. In most of his pamphlets, which were written in the seventeenth century, Dekker seems to have learned most from the style of Greene's later pamphlets.

Thomas Kyd, some six years older than Marlowe, collaborated with him in 1591; but this play has apparently not survived. His extant work is of various kinds: a pamphlet about a contemporary murder trial, a prose translation from Tasso, a very beautiful translation of a French Senecan play—Garnier's *Cornelia*—and several plays of his own. He is thought by some to be the author of the impressive domestic tragedy *Arden of Feversham*; and he is thought by many to be the author of the original *Hamlet*. He may be the author of *Soliman and Perseda,* a condensed version of which is used at the end of *The Spanish Tragedy*. But it is *The Spanish Tragedy* on which Kyd's reputation as a dramatist largely depends since it is the one play of undisputed authorship. It remained one of the most popular Elizabethan plays, and it was revised more than once, after Kyd's death, by other dramatists. One addition to the play, first printed in 1602, is a magnificent prose scene between Hieronimo and a painter, so splendid in its depiction of madness that Jonson, Webster, Dekker, and even Shakespeare have been credited with its authorship.

The importance of *The Spanish Tragedy* in the development of Elizabethan drama can hardly be overestimated. Written probably about 1590, before the best plays of Greene and Marlowe, it has a complex and well-constructed plot, and scenes full of action and violence. In one sense it can be regarded as a Senecan play converted to the popular Elizabethan stage, with a ghost as prologue and revenge as its theme. It is generally regarded as the first Elizabethan revenge play, a genre that culminated in *Hamlet* and some of the greatest Jacobean plays; but in a recent essay Professor G. K. Hunter has argued that if it is regarded as a revenge play it "shows up as rather a botched piece of work." [6] He declares that it is "not centrally concerned with the enactment of revenge" but rather with the question of justice, the play being "the inheritor of a complex and rich tradition of moralizing dramaturgy." This interpretation has the merit of explaining the function both of the early scenes and of the subplot. But, of course, all revenge plays, including *Hamlet,* are concerned with the relation of revenge to justice; all of them are concerned with the workings of providence, as well as with the actions of men; and in nearly all of them the successful avenger is himself destroyed.

The original audiences doubtless enjoyed the blood-and-thunder elements in the play: the ghost, the discovery of Horatio's murder, Hieronimo's madness and the biting out of his tongue, and the sequence of events conveniently summarized by the satisfied ghost of Andrea:

> Horatio murder'd in his father's bower,
> Vild Serberine by Pedringano slain,
> False Pedringano hanged by quaint device,
> Fair Isabella by herself misdone,
> Prince Balthazar by Bel-imperia stabbed,
> The Duke of Castile and his wicked son
> Both done to death by old Hieronimo,
> My Bel-imperia fallen as Dido fell,
> And good Hieronimo slain by himself:
> Ay, these were spectacles to please my soul.

[6] *Renaissance Drama,* ed. S. Schoenbaum (Evanston, Ill.: Northwestern Univ. Press, 1966), VIII, p. 89.

They were also spectacles to please the soul of the audience. But it would be a mistake to suppose that the continued popularity of the play, which survived numerous parodies and imitations, was due entirely, or even mainly, to the high death roll and to the numerous horrors. We know from the parodies themselves that the age was fascinated by Kyd's rhetorical dexterity, as they had been by Lyly's; and Kyd's verse has much greater variety than Lyly's prose. The elaborate patterned speech could be used to illustrate many of the figures described in textbooks of rhetoric. In this passage, for example, each successive line picks up a word from the previous one:

> First in his hand he brandished a sword,
> And with that sword he fiercely waged war,
> And in that war he gave me dangerous wounds,
> And by those wounds he forced me to yield,
> And by my yielding I became his slave.

The most famous passage in the play is Hieronimo's soliloquy. Artificial and often ridiculed, it is, in its way, superb:

> O eyes, no eyes, but fountains frought with tears;
> O life, no life, but lively form of death;
> O world, no world, but mass of public wrongs,
> Confused and filled with murder and misdeeds!
> O sacred heavens, if this unhallowed deed,
> If this inhuman and barbarous attempt,
> If this incomparable murder thus
> Of mine, but now no more my son,
> Shall unrevealed and unrevenged pass,
> How should we term your dealings to be just,
> If you unjustly deal with those that in your justice trust?

In the lines he wrote on Shakespeare for inclusion in

the First Folio, Jonson proclaimed how far his dead friend

> didst our Lyly outshine.
> Or sporting Kyd, or Marlowe's mighty line.

Shakespeare learned from all these dramatists, and also from Greene; and in the fields in which they each excelled he surpassed them all. But, without their pioneering work, he would have taken longer to develop his own style and technique.

Kyd died soon after Greene and Marlowe, and Lyly ceased to write plays. In the middle nineties Shakespeare was left without a serious rival. There were a number of minor playwrights whose stature is difficult to assess as so much of their work has not survived. Antony Munday was not without talent, and at least one of Henry Porter's plays, *The Two Angry Women of Abington,* is a lively comedy. There were some good anonymous plays, such as *Edward III,* to which Shakespeare may have contributed a scene or two, as he certainly did to the banned play on Sir Thomas More by Munday and others.

Toward the end of the century the new wave of dramatists began to emerge. Ben Jonson's first good play, *Every Man in His Humour,* was performed by Shakespeare's company in 1598; George Chapman's first "humor" comedies appeared before 1599; John Marston turned to the stage when his satires were banned and wrote the first of his interesting but unsatisfactory plays, *Antonio and Mellida*; and Thomas Dekker, who had been writing for some years, emerged as a considerable dramatist with the rollicking character of Simon Eyre in *The Shoemaker's Holiday.*

In the induction to *Every Man Out of His Humour* Jonson described the theory on which he based his comic method:

> In every human body
> The choler, melancholy, phlegm and blood,
> By reason that they flow continually
> In some one part, and are not continent,
> Receive the name of humours. Now thus far
> It may by metaphor, apply itself
> Unto the general disposition:
> As when some one peculiar quality
> Doth so possess a man that it doth draw
> All his affects, his spirits and his powers
> In their confluctions all to run one way,
> This may be truly said to be a humour.

The comedy of humors was thus based on the physiological theory of the four humors corresponding to the four elements, the character being determined by their proportion and balance in a man's constitution. But the significant words in the lines quoted above are "by metaphor." Jonson's comedy does not depend on the validity of the physiological theory. By "humor" he meant (in Dryden's words) "some extravagant habit, passion or affection [i.e., affectation], particular to some one person, by the oddness of which he is immediately distinguished from the rest of men." [7] The effect of the theory was to make Jonson's characters types, since in real life no one can be described in terms of a single eccentricity. But on the stage such simplification can be remarkably effective: the boasting of Bobadil, the melancholy of Stephen in *Every Man in His Humour,* Morose's hatred of noise in *The Silent Woman.*

In his great comedies, written in the reign of King

[7] *Of Dramatic Poesy* (1665).

James, Jonson was not bound too closely by his theory; and such characters as Volpone, Sir Politic Would-be, Sir Epicure Mammon, and Zeal-of-the-Land Busy are much more than mere humors. Shakespeare himself, at the turn of the century, seems to have been influenced by the comedy of humors, especially in his minor characters. But even in Malvolio and Jaques we may discern the humors of self-love and melancholy.

Suggested Reading

Marlowe's plays are available in several editions, e.g., Tucker Brooke (Oxford: Clarendon Press, 1910) and L. Kirschbaum (Cleveland, Ohio: World Publishing Co., 1962). Editions of individual plays include *Doctor Faustus* by W. W. Greg (Oxford: Clarendon Press, 1950) and by J. D. Jump (London: Methuen, 1962); *Edward II* by Charlton and Waller (London: Methuen, rev. 1955); *Tamburlaine* by U. Ellis-Fermor (London: Methuen, 1930); *The Jew of Malta* by R. Van Fossen (Lincoln: Univ. of Nebraska Press, 1965). There is a useful collection of essays on his work edited by C. Leech (Englewood Cliffs, N. J.: Prentice-Hall, 1964). Recent critical works include *The Overreacher* by H. Levin (Cambridge, Mass.: Harvard Univ. Press, 1952); *Suffering and Evil in the Plays of Christopher Marlowe* by D. Cole (Princeton Univ. Press, 1962); *Marlowe* by J. B. Steane (Cambridge Univ. Press, 1964).

Some plays by Greene, Peele, Lyly, and Kyd are included in *Minor Elizabethan Drama,* edited by A. Thorndike (London: Dent, 1910). The standard edition of Greene's plays is the unsatisfactory one by J. C. Collins (Oxford: Clarendon Press, 1905). A number of his pamphlets were edited by G. B. Harrison in the Bodley Head quartos (London, 1923), who also edited the best of his novels, *Menaphon* (Oxford: Blackwell, 1927). *Pandosto* was edited by P. G. Thomas (London: Chatto and Windus, 1907).

The only modern edition of Peele's work is by C. T. Prouty and others (New Haven, Conn.: Yale Univ. Press

1952–   ). R. B. McKerrow's great edition of Nashe was revised by F. P. Wilson (Oxford: Blackwell, 1958). There is a good selection by Stanley Wells (London: Arnold, 1964) and a study, *Thomas Nashe,* by G. R. Hibbard (London: Routledge and Kegan Paul, 1962).

R. W. Bond's edition of Lyly (Oxford: Clarendon Press, 1902) is being replaced by G. K. Hunter, the author of the best book on the subject, *John Lyly: The Humanist as Courtier* (London: Routledge and Kegan Paul, 1962).

The works of Lodge, excluding the translations, were edited by Edmund Gosse (Glasgow: Hunterian Society, 1883). Bernard Shaw began, but did not complete the index of this edition. *Rosalynde* has often been reprinted and is now available in G. Bullough's *Narrative and Dramatic Sources of Shakespeare,* Vol. II (New York: Columbia Univ. Press, 1958).

The only complete edition of Kyd is by F. S. Boas (Oxford: Clarendon Press, 1901). There is a good edition of *The Spanish Tragedy* by Philip Edwards (London: Methuen, 1959).

Jonson's complete works were edited by C. H. Herford and P. Simpson (Oxford: Clarendon Press, 1925–52); but the plays alone, edited by F. E. Schelling, are available in Everyman's Library (London: Dent, 1910). There is a good selection, *Five Plays,* in *The World's Classics* (Oxford Univ. Press, 1953).

Dekker's plays have been edited by F. Bowers without annotation (Cambridge Univ. Press, 1953–61). *The Shoemaker's Holiday* is included in *Six Elizabethan Plays,* edited by C. B. Wheeler (Oxford Univ. Press, n.d.).

Marston's poems were edited by A. Davenport (Liverpool Univ. Press, 1961) and his plays by H. Harvey Wood (Edinburgh: Oliver and Boyd, 1934–39). *Antonio and Mellida* and *Antonio's Revenge* have been edited by G. K. Hunter (Lincoln: Univ. of Nebraska Press, 1965).

Porter's *The Two Angry Women of Abington* is included in C. M. Gayley's *Representative English Comedies* (New York: Macmillan, 1903). Two of Munday's plays have been published by the Malone Society, *John a Kent and John a Cumber* (1923) and *The Downfall of Robert, Earl of Huntingdon* (1965).

VIII
The Elizabethan Shakespeare

William Shakespeare (b. 1564) probably left his native Stratford-upon-Avon in 1584. We next hear of him, already established as an actor and playwright, in 1592, when the dying Robert Greene told his fellows the University Wits that their day was past, since the actors now had their own dramatist, a "shake-scene," a "Johannes factotum," a jack-of-all-trades, Shakespeare. How the poet spent the seven intervening years is not known, although soldier, sailor, solicitor's clerk, "a schoolmaster in the country," and many other occupations have been suggested. It seems most likely that he was learning his job as an actor and beginning to write plays. In 1592, with the publication of *Venus and Adonis,* he became the most popular poet of his time; and two years later, when he reached the age of thirty, he had some eight plays and two narrative poems to his credit.

It used to be thought that Shakespeare began his career as a dramatist by revising the work of other men; but the only serious evidence that he revised other men's plays belongs to a later date. He wrote two scenes in the censored play *Sir Thomas More*; he based *Hamlet* and *King Lear* and possibly *The Merry Wives of Windsor* and *Much Ado about Nothing* on earlier plays; and if we compare the later acts with the first two of *Pericles,* we can see him at work. But all these tasks were carried out when he was an established dramatist. There is no real evidence that *Henry VI* was based on the work of Marlowe, Greene, and Peele; and the resemblances between their work and Shakespeare's may best be explained by the probability that he evolved a style of his own by imitating those of his contemporaries, as Keats imitated Hunt.

The three parts of *Henry VI* constituted a new dramatic form, the chronicle history, which Shakespeare seems to have invented. The three plays together are a kind of epic drama without a hero. They cover a span of fifty years, from the death of Henry V to the murder of his successor. The central action is concerned with the Wars of the Roses, a civil strife that can be traced back to the deposition of Richard II and that results in the loss of France. The action is not resolved until the sequel, when the marriage of Richmond at the end of *Richard III* unites the houses of Lancaster and York. Shakespeare was dealing with a period not far removed

from his own—Richmond's granddaughter was on the
throne—and the fear of civil war had received a new
impetus from rebellions in the reigns of all five Tudors.
These had all been suppressed without difficulty because of the power of the central government, which
had been so conspicuously lacking in the reign of
Henry VI.

Shakespeare had set himself a difficult task. It was
impossible to present a whole series of battles without
the risk of monotony; although every scene could con-
tribute to the main theme, it was impossible to have
more than an episodic plot; and the size of the cast, some
forty speaking parts in each of the three plays, meant
that the interest was liable to be dissipated. The last
difficulty was increased by Shakespeare's immaturity as a
dramatist. He did not yet possess the power of creating
a character in a few lines or of seeming to speak through
the mouths of even his most minor characters. In addition, the style of acting prevalent in Shakespeare's early
years was declamatory rather than naturalistic. In many
scenes of *Henry VI* the characters seem to orate to each
other, and there is little attempt to differentiate the
speech of one character from that of another, so that
even a sea captain can describe the nightfall after a sea
battle in these terms:

> The gaudy, blabbing and remorseful day
> Is crept into the bosom of the sea;
> And now loud-howling wolves arouse the jades
> That drag the tragic melancholy night . . .

Some of the best scenes are frankly unnaturalistic, as
when King Henry soliloquizes at the Battle of Towton
and watches a son who has slain his father, and a father

who has slain his son. The scene symbolizes plainly the tragedy of civil war.

Yet, in the course of writing the trilogy, Shakespeare gradually learned the successful presentation of character. Warwick, Margaret, and Henry become, in the end, three-dimensional. Above all, the melodramatic Glouces-ter is full of vitality. Shakespeare in this character learned something from Marlowe's sardonic villain-heroes, but he went beyond his master. Despite the ob-vious immaturity of the trilogy, several stage produc-tions in recent years have demonstrated its power to hold an audience and how unnecessary it is to adapt it for the modern stage, as was done at Stratford-upon-Avon in 1964.

In *Richard III,* Shakespeare, using the same kind of historical material, contrived to weld it into a real unity by concentrating on the rise and fall of his protagonist. It is a beautifully constructed play, with each scene di-rectly relevant to the main action. Even the survival of apparently primitive technique has a dramatic point. The ritualistic cursing of the women in Act IV and the chorus of ghosts in Act V direct our sympathies and prevent us from siding with the protagonist because of his cleverness and gusto. On the eve of the Battle of Bosworth, after the appearance of the ghosts, Richard's realization that his earlier boast, "I am myself alone," is a mark of his damnation, comes too late, perhaps, to transform melodrama into tragedy, but the character, with this limitation, is presented with extraordinary mastery. The verse, especially in Richard's opening soliloquy and Clarence's dream, has a greater flexibility than in most of *Henry VI*; the characters, except in the scenes of ritual, converse rather than declaim; and Shakespeare reveals a sardonic humor he never afterward fully exploited.

Richard III was more successful than the only unhistorical tragedy of Shakespeare's early years. *Titus Andronicus* is a blood-and-thunder melodrama in which the hero, maddened by the death of his son and the rape and mutilation of his daughter, avenges himself on Tamora by serving up her sons to her baked in a pie. Some of the scenes are powerful, and the villainous Moor, Aaron, is well drawn. The horrors are qualified to some extent, as Eugene Waith has shown, by the Ovidian conceits of the verse in which they are described. Shakespeare endeavors to arouse pity and terror by piling on the horrors, probably under the bad influence of Seneca, but the play remains his one undoubted failure.

Meanwhile Shakespeare had been experimenting with several kinds of comedy. In *The Comedy of Errors,* adapted from the *Menaechmi,* he goes one better than Plautus, providing his twins with twin servants, and thereby multiplying the opportunities for mistaken identity; and he borrowed the idea for one scene from another comedy of Plautus, the *Amphytrion.* This farcical plot Shakespeare sets in a tragicomic framework, with the father of the twins separated from wife and children and about to be executed. Shakespeare was never content with pure farce because he could never exclude genuine human feeling from his work. Adriana's jealousy, not altogether unjustified, enabled the dramatist to examine the nature of marriage; and, by providing Adriana with a sister, he was able to supply a bride for the unmarried Antipholus. The plotting is brilliant, but the play is prevented from being a masterpiece by the rhymed doggerel used in some of the scenes. This is thought by some critics to be a survival from an earlier play. It is more likely to be a mistaken adherence to tradition on Shakespeare's part, for the same kind of verse had been used in the first English imitation of Plautus, *Ralph Roister Doister*.

The Taming of the Shrew combines a farcical story of wife-taming with a plot based on Ariosto's comedy, translated by Gascoigne as *Supposes*; and the play is supposed to be performed before the tinker, Christopher Sly, who awakens from his drunken sleep to find himself dressed and treated as a lord. The plots are linked together by the fact that the two heroines are sisters, and their father will not allow Bianca to be married until Katherine the Shrew is off his hands. In the wager scene at the end Katherine proves to be more obedient than her demure sister. The story of a swaggering fortune hunter who tames his bride, as though she were a hawk, by starving her, could be a rather brutal farce. Shakespeare prevents it from being that by convincing us that, despite appearances, Petruchio and Katherine are in love; that her shrewishness is due partly to her knowledge that the favorite Bianca is a sly puss, partly to her revulsion from marriages of convenience, and partly to her unconscious desire to be mastered by a man she can respect. The homily she addresses to the other wives on the necessity of obedience, however unpleasing to married ears today, remained orthodox teaching until long after Shakespeare's day. In spite of the ingenuity of the Bianca plot, the characters in it are comparatively colorless and the verse sometimes rather weak. This has led some critics to suppose that these scenes are a survival from an earlier play. But one gets a similar contrast in *Much Ado About Nothing* between the vitality of the Beatrice-Benedick scenes and the more conventional Hero-Claudio plot. In both cases the contrast may have been deliberate.

The third of the early comedies, *The Two Gentlemen of Verona,* based, though not necessarily directly, on an episode in Montemayor's *Diana,* is the least popular of the three on the modern stage, though it is closer in form and spirit to Shakespeare's mature comedies than either of the other two. It contains better poetry than either; the characterization is more subtle; by means of soliloquies we are given more insight into the minds of the main characters; and it contains one of Shakespeare's funniest clowns, Launce. For a modern audience all goes well until the last scene, when Proteus, who has deserted his first love and caused his friend Valentine to be outlawed, finally tries to rape Valentine's love, Silvia. He is foiled by the appearance of Valentine; he asks forgiveness of his friend, which the latter not only grants, but then proposes to relinquish Silvia to Proteus:

> By penitence the Eternal's wrath's appeased:
> And that my love may appear plain and free,
> All that was mine in Silvia I give thee.

Julia, who is present disguised as a page, swoons. Silvia, not unnaturally, is rendered speechless for the rest of the play. It is assumed by some critics that the scene is textually corrupt—the play was not published until at least thirty years after its first performance. Other critics believe that Shakespeare was arguing, as in the *Sonnets,* for the superior claims of friendship over love. But it is one thing for a man to give up a woman to a friend, where the man is noble and the woman willing, and another to hand over a woman who loves him to her would-be ravisher. Shakespeare must have been conscious of the absurdity of the situation, and he was presumably satirizing the fashionable cult of friendship, as elsewhere in the play he satirizes romantic love through the mouth of his clowns and by the behavior of Sir Thurio and Sir Eglamour, the one a poltroon and the other a singularly ineffective knight-errant.

There is disguise or mistaken identity in every one of Shakespeare's comedies, and Julia is the first of many heroines—Portia, Rosalind, Viola, Imogen—who disguises herself as a boy; and she is sent by the man she loves to visit her rival. This kind of disguise was, of course, a natural expedient in the Elizabethan theater, in which all the roles were played by men.

The three comedies we have discussed are well constructed, and it has been argued that Shakespeare must have studied the plot structure of Latin comedy. The fourth comedy, however, *Love's Labour's Lost,* almost dispenses with plot. All that happens in the main action is that the four men who vow to see no women for a year fall in love with the first women who invade their solitude. The climax of the play, in which each of the vow-breakers is exposed in turn, is a magnificent tour de force; and Berowne's defense of their perjury is the finest dramatic poetry that Shakespeare had written up to this time.

The play is filled out with a group of minor characters who perform the Pageant of the Nine Worthies at the end of the play. These are partly based on stock

figures in the commedia dell'arte but some of these also
appear to satirize contemporaries of Shakespeare. Holo-
fernes, the schoolmaster, is in some sense a satirical
portrait of John Florio, afterward famous as the translator of Montaigne; Armado has been identified with
Ralegh and Antonio Perez; Boyet with Chapman; and
Moth with Nashe. It is therefore assumed that the play
was originally written not for the public theater, but
for a private audience who would appreciate the personal satire. The exact point of some speeches in the
play is now lost irrecoverably; but the satire on ped-
antry, on affectations of speech, and, above all, on the
noblemen who propose to banish women from their ideal
republic is still as fresh and amusing as ever. The minor
characters are richly absurd; Berowne is the wittiest and
most eloquent of Shakespeare's early heroes; the Nine
Worthies are still extremely funny; and the songs are
exquisite. One of the most successful strokes in the play
is near the end, when the arrival of the messenger to
announce the death of the Princess' father introduces a
note of reality and prepares the way for the penances
imposed on the nobles for their pride, their self-sufficiency, their broken vows, and their failure to understand either themselves or the world.

By this time Shakespeare had written two of his narrative poems and some of his sonnets. *Venus and Adonis,*
which Shakespeare described as the first heir of his invention (i.e., his first published work), was based on the
Ovidian tale of Venus' love for the mortal Adonis, who
is slain by a boar. As Adonis rejects the advances of the
goddess, we can hardly assume that Shakespeare intended the boar to symbolize lust, as in some other treat-

ments of the story. Nor can it be said that the moral of
the poem is the contrast between love and lust,

> Love comforteth like sunshine after rain,
> But Lust's effect is tempest after sun,

since our sympathies are mainly with Venus and since
Adonis rejects her, not on moral grounds but because he
is guilty of pride and self-sufficiency. Nor, indeed, is it
possible to agree with those critics who believe that the
poem is comic throughout or those others who regard it
as effeminate, artificial, heartless, bookish, obscene, and
disgusting.

Shakespeare's imagination was essentially dramatic,
and he was able to view the situation through the eyes of
both his protagonists and to sympathize with both. We
are made to feel the full force of Venus' arguments for
love, as well as the reluctance of the unawakened adoles-
cent. But Shakespeare shows, too, that both characters
use reason to defend an irrational position.

Some of the imagery and description in the poem are
drawn from books—and this is a characteristic of Shakespeare's imagery to the end of his career—but if we
did not know that the description of the boar was lifted
from Ovid, we might assume it was based on observation. The total effect is not one of bookishness, and
many of the descriptions are taken from nature. In one
respect, as Coleridge pointed out, the poem shows the
promise of greatness: the images are not merely copied
faithfully from nature; they are "modified by a pre-
dominant passion," and "a human and intellectual life
is transferred to them from the poet's own spirit." [1]

---

[1] *Biographia Literaria*, XV.

But it is clear from the epistle dedicatory that Shakespeare did not intend his erotic poem to be taken too seriously. He there promises "a graver labour"; and *Lucrece* was published in the following year. In this poem all our sympathies are with the ravished heroine, though the conflict in the mind of Tarquin between lust and honor is powerfully presented. The poem is more dramatic than *Venus and Adonis,* and it looks forward to Shakespeare's mature tragedies. It is written in rhyme royal, the stanza used by Chaucer in *Troilus and Criseyde,* and it has a slower, graver movement than the six-line stanza of *Venus and Adonis.* Shakespeare took immense pains with its composition, and it would be possible to use it to illustrate many rhetorical figures. It is, indeed, better than the "complaints" of Spenser and Daniel, and Lucrece's lament is, in its way, magnificent. Coleridge rightly said that the poem showed that Shakespeare possessed "a most profound, energetic and philosophical mind." [2] Yet most readers find it something of a disappointment after *Venus and Adonis*: it lacks some of the freshness and sensuous brilliance of the earlier poem; it is more "literary," and more labored.

A third narrative poem, *A Lover's Complaint,* published with the *Sonnets,* is so much weaker than the other two that attempts have been made to deny Shakespeare's authorship. It is, perhaps, an unfinished draft; but there is no reason to suppose that Shakespeare was not responsible for it.

The *Sonnets* were not published until 1609, but they were probably written in the decade after the publication of *Astrophel and Stella,* when almost every poet was

[2] *Ibid.*

writing sonnets. Most of Shakespeare's were written to a young aristocrat, in the early ones urging him to marry, in the later ones expressing a friendship that was sometimes threatened by rival poets and sometimes by the seduction of the young man by Shakespeare's mistress. A group of sonnets at the end is addressed to the Dark Lady, and in them the poet contrasts his adulterous passion with his pure love for his friend. The sequence is unlikely to be fictitious since the sonnets in that case would have been arranged to tell a more coherent story. On the other hand, it would be dangerous to assume that the poet stuck rigidly to the actual events of his relationship. There is probably an element of dramatization.

Not all the sonnets are successful. In some the concluding couplet seems perfunctory; others are smart and overingenious; a few, toward the end of the main sequence, read like dutiful exercises. But, when all is said, and despite the poet's separation of the sexual appetite and love, the collection as a whole reveals Shakespeare as the best love poet in the language, as the poet of unselfish and disinterested love. He is singularly clear-sighted, both in analyzing his own enslavement to the Dark Lady and in gently reproving the faults of his friend. When he boasts of the immortality of his poetry,

Not marble nor the gilded monuments
Of princes shall outlive this powerful rhyme,

it is solely because he wishes to immortalize his friend. The main theme of the sequence is the threat to beauty and love by time. The first way of defeating this threat is by marriage so that the friend's beauty will be passed down to his children. Later on, this solution is forgotten;

and, with the deepening of his friendship, the poet hopes to cheat time by means of his poetry. In the end, realizing that his love is not fully reciprocated and that beauty of person does not guarantee beauty of character, Shakespeare proclaims that, whatever happens, his love is not subject to time:

> Let me not to the marriage of true minds
> Admit impediments. Love is not love
> Which alters when it alteration finds,
> Or bends with the remover to remove.
> O, no! it is an ever-fixed mark
> That looks on tempests and is never shaken;
> It is the star to every wandering bark
> Whose worth's unknown although his height be taken.
> Love's not Time's fool, though rosy lips and cheeks
> Within his bending sickle's compass come;
> Love alters not with his brief hours and weeks
> But bears it out even to the edge of doom.
>   If this be error and upon me proved,
>   I never writ, nor no man ever loved.

Meanwhile Shakespeare had written of a reciprocated love in his first tragic masterpiece, *Romeo and Juliet*. The protagonists come from rival factions, and they are destroyed as a result of the feud, but their deaths reconcile the families. They are dogged by misfortune: Romeo is compelled to fight Juliet's cousin, Tybalt, on the very day of his marriage; the messenger sent to Romeo in exile is delayed by the plague; and Juliet awakens from her trance just too late to prevent the suicide of her husband. The total effect of the play is therefore pathetic rather than tragic, and Shakespeare never afterward relied so much on accident. Some critics, indeed, have sought to show that the lovers are largely responsible for their own misfortunes because they allow passion to usurp the place of reason and because of their alacrity in suicide. But their secret marriage is arranged by Friar Lawrence, as is also the device of the sleeping potion, and he is blamed by no one. The suicide of the lovers may be regarded as an error, but most members of an audience would shrink from condemning an act that reveals the lovers' generous and total commitment to each other.

In several respects *Romeo and Juliet* marks a great advance. The characterization, particularly of Mercutio, Juliet, and the nurse, is more subtle than in the previous plays; and this is partly due to a greater flexibility in the verse, which enables the poet to give the illusion of colloquial speech. Second, Shakespeare was exploiting fully for the first time the characteristics of the Elizabethan stage, in the balcony scene, for example. Third, the actual poetry in the best scenes has a force and beauty that Shakespeare had not previously achieved. Last, in *Romeo and Juliet,* and in the other plays written in 1595, he used for the first time the device of iterative imagery, images drawn from particular fields, which create the required atmosphere or illuminate the theme of the play. In this case there is a great deal of imagery drawn from religion, and many images concerned with explosions and lightning in a dark night.

Probably in the same year Shakespeare began his second historical tetralogy with *Richard II. King John,* which belongs to neither tetralogy, may have been written earlier; but from the maturity of some of the verse it appears to have been revised later. Shakespeare had dramatized the Wars of the Roses. Now he turned to the ultimate cause of those wars in the deposition and murder of Richard II. He had several advantages he had not possessed when he wrote *Henry VI*: the actual historical material could more easily be given dramatic shape—there had, in fact, been plays on the reign before Shakespeare wrote his; Marlowe had demonstrated in *Edward II* how the facts of history could be turned into formal tragedy; and Shakespeare's own dramatic powers had matured. The basic opposition in the play is between the rightful king, interesting as a man but a bad ruler, and the usurper, who is a good ruler. Shakespeare sharpens this opposition by stressing the divine right of kings through the mouth of Richard himself and by means of the powerful speech of the Bishop of Carlisle in the deposition scene. But we know that Richard has been guilty of murder, and in the course of the play he seizes Gaunt's property and thus provides Bolingbroke with an excuse for returning from exile. Bolingbroke, moreover, is not an obvious villain. He moves step by step from claiming his rights to seizing the throne. Once he has defied the King by returning from banishment, he can safeguard his position only by usurpation. He is given no soliloquies, so we never know how conscious he is of what he is doing or whether he was aiming at the crown from the start.

Until Richard's return from Ireland all our sympathies are with the victims of his misgovernment. Thereafter we are gradually drawn to sympathize with Richard in his misfortune, partly because of a natural tendency to pity those who fall from high estate and partly because of the magnificent poetry Shakespeare puts into his mouth. In the deposition scene his very theatricality plays on our feelings; the scene in which he parts from his wife, the account of the ride into London, the incident of the faithful groom, and his desperate last fight all evoke our pity; and his soliloquy in prison, in which he acknowledges his misgovernment, completes the reversal of our sympathies. Yet he is not so much changed that we cannot see the continuity between the man who interrupts the fight in the first act and the man who suffers in the last.

When Shakespeare turned to dramatize the next reign he had to find a new means of hammering his material into shape. An old play, *The Famous Victories of Henry V*, with its account of Hal's youthful escapades, provided one model. The two parts of *Henry IV* are partly concerned with the evolution of the madcap Prince into the successful King. This is shown by his defeat of Hotspur at the end of Part I and his rejection of Falstaff at the end of Part II. In this respect *Henry IV* is a kind of prologue to *Henry V*. But it is also a continuation of *Richard II,* and we are shown the results of Bolingbroke's usurpation. The new King is troubled with feelings of guilt, which he hopes to expiate by a crusade to the Holy Land, and with a series of rebellions. Part I is complete in itself, with the rivalry between Hal and Hotspur settled at the Battle of Shrewsbury and the King convinced of his son's reformation; and there are signs in Part II that Shakespeare was seriously short of historical matter to fill out the play. He solved the problem by showing what had previously been described, Falstaff's recruiting activities, and by making the King have renewed doubts about his son.

Part I has been considered as a satirical comedy on war and policy, with the main action parodied in the subplot. The Battle of Shrewsbury is taken off in advance by the robbery at Gadshill; Henry IV's solemn interview with his son is preceded by the scene in which Falstaff and Hal both assume the King's role; and the battle itself is interspersed with Falstaff's cynical comments and behavior. The rebels quarrel about the division of the country before they have fought a battle, and though the King's own position is based on crime, the rebels are motivated not by a desire to set the rightful king on the throne, but entirely by self-interest. Hotspur's gospel of honor is undermined by Falstaff's soliloquy on the subject.

This interpretation, true as far as it goes, leaves out of consideration other aspects of the play, which are at least as important: the Prince being trained for kingship by getting to know the world and by learning to reject the irresponsible and anarchic elements in his own character at the call of duty, and the dramatic rivalry between Hal, the man who is able to control his passions, and Hotspur, who, in spite of his attractive qualities, never does.

Part II is more somber in tone. The feigned illness of Northumberland and his hysterical outburst when he hears of the death of his son, the dying King suffering from insomnia, the senility of Justice Shallow, and the gout and pox that attack the aging Falstaff combine to give the impression of a sick kingdom. The treacherous arrest of the rebels by Prince John brings out the sordid realities of Machiavellian policy. Falstaff, moreover, is shown in a more sordid light. We knew that he was a glutton, a drunkard, a cheat, and a whoremonger; but in Part II we watch him cheating Mistress Quickly, embezzling in Gloucestershire, and consorting with Doll Tearsheet. This was dramatically necessary to prepare the way for his rejection in the last act.

In spite of this preparation, some good critics have felt uneasy about the scene of Falstaff's rejection. It was necessary for Prince Hal to repudiate his old associates, necessary even for him to do it publicly as a matter of policy; but the tone in which he does it is unnecessarily smug. It is a measure of Shakespeare's brilliant portrayal of Falstaff, with whom and at whom we have laughed, that we cannot help liking him more than the nominal hero of the play. Shakespeare's greatest comic character is a combination of several different elements: he is partly the braggart soldier of Latin comedy, partly the Vice of the Moralities, partly the Lollard Oldcastle (a name that Shakespeare was forced to alter), and partly the Lord of Misrule. He has to be witty, humorous, and attractive, as he would not otherwise be a serious temptation. Hal, in rejecting him, prepares himself for his role as the victor of Agincourt; but he loses some of his humanity in the process.

The Eastcheap and Gloucestershire scenes are written in prose, though in a prose further removed from actual colloquial speech than that of Jonson, Middleton, or Dekker. It is significant, perhaps, that Shakespeare's most vital characters in the plays written at this time— Shylock, Beatrice, Rosalind, and Falstaff—all speak mainly in prose. It was not until *Julius Caesar* and *Hamlet* that he solved the problem of writing verse as natural as prose. This does not mean that he appears handicapped in the verse scenes of *Henry IV*. The verse in which Hotspur speaks brilliantly conveys the man;

and in Part II the verse is almost as powerful and as eloquently varied as that of the great tragedies.

Between *Henry IV* and *Henry V,* Shakespeare, apparently at the Queen's request, showed Falstaff in love, in a farce set in Elizabethan times, *The Merry Wives of Windsor,* which was probably a hurried adaptation of an earlier play. Theatrically, it is brilliant; but the central character shares only a name and obesity with the fat knight who bestrides the two parts of *Henry IV* like a colossus. Shakespeare wisely kept Falstaff out of the epic drama *Henry V*; but Mistress Quickly's account of his death, broken-hearted, is the scene in that play that most touches the heart, with its combination of malapropism and pathos.

Henry V is a workmanlike rounding off of the tetralogy. It is a patriotic celebration of the hero of Agincourt, full of stirring rhetoric, and rising to an impressive climax when the disguised King wanders through the apparently doomed camp. There is a fine debate on war guilt and an amusing wooing scene in which the King, to the delight of the groundlings, no doubt, poses as a simple soldier. Some modern critics have hopefully suggested that, although Shakespeare was giving the public what it wanted, he had ironies and reservations about his hero. If so, the only scene in which they come to the surface is the one in which the clergy, anxious for the King's support in their quarrel with Parliament, pronounce that he is the rightful ruler of France.

This concluded Shakespeare's sequence of plays on English history, apart from *Henry VIII* at the very end of his career. But during the years when he was writing the second tetralogy he had established himself as the unrivaled master of comedy. *A Midsummer Night's Dream,* like *Love's Labour's Lost,* was written for a private audience, in celebration of a wedding; and it expands one device from the previous play: the performance of an entertainment by incompetent amateurs before a courtly audience. "Pyramus and Thisbe" showed intelligent members of the audience that *Romeo and Juliet,* written just before, had depended too much on accident; it would amuse the sophisticated by the contrast between the Ovidian original and the burlesque; and it would show that lovers cannot always rely on the intervention of Oberon to save them from the consequences of their own irrationality. For Puck's magic juice only underlines the irrational element in romantic love; and the play, with its four cunningly interwoven plots, is a delicate satire. Not only do the four central characters change partners with bewildering rapidity; Oberon is irrationally jealous of Titania, and she comes to love an ass. Bottom wisely comments that "reason and love keep little company together now-a-days," and Puck exclaims, with reason: "Lord! What fools these mortals be!" Even the mature Theseus has sown his wild oats, but we are meant to suppose that the "everlasting bond of fellowship" with Hippolyta will be durable. Shakespeare is contrasting romantic love with the more rational and constant love of matrimony.

It is usually assumed that Theseus, in his famous comparison of the lunatic, the lover, and the poet, is acting as Shakespeare's spokesman. But Shakespeare, as we know from the *Sonnets,* did not see "Helen's beauty in a brow of Egypt." As a lover he was not anesthetized by the imagination; and as a poet he knew the difference between the disordered imagination of the lunatic, reflecting only illusion, and the creative imagination of the poet, which reflected reality. Theseus, moreover, is wrong even about the story of the lovers, for in the world of the play it actually happened.

The play ends with three marriages and the reconciliation of Oberon and Titania. The fairies bless the marriage beds of the couples in the play and, by implication, the newly married couple in the audience. There are two other ways by which the play is linked with the actual world: the speech about the Queen, "the fair vestal throned in the west," and the long description of the bad summer that, it is suggested, has been caused by the quarrel between Oberon and Titania.

There are no villains in Shakespeare's early comedies; but in those written in the last years of the sixteenth century, the threat to a happy ending comes from external evil. Shylock, Don John, and Oliver are manifestly wicked, although Oliver repents in the last act.

The theme of *The Merchant of Venice* was doubtless suggested to Shakespeare by the trial of Dr. Lopez in 1594 on a false charge of attempting to poison Queen Elizabeth and by the success of the revival of Marlowe's *The Jew of Malta*. Shakespeare was in advance of his age in recognizing that Shylock's evil was partly the result of his treatment by the Christians. Even Antonio spits on his gaberdine. Shakespeare condemns Shylock for his usury and murderous intentions; but he also condemns by implication the racial prejudice of the Christians. It is not Shylock's race that is condemned, for Lorenzo cheerfully marries Jessica, but his Jewish faith and his

evil conduct. In a famous speech Shylock shows that
Christians share with Jews a common humanity ("hath
not a Jew eyes?"), and Portia, too, at the trial stresses
the common element in their religion:

> We all do pray for mercy, and that same prayer
> Should teach us all to render deeds of mercy.

On the other hand, it is misreading the play to assume,
as some have done, that the Christians are a rotten lot
and that Bassanio, the fortune hunter, would never have
chosen the leaden casket. He is the dashing prodigal
who inevitably wins the hand of the princess. The
caskets with their inscriptions are nicely designed to
eliminate unsuitable suitors—those who are after Portia's fortune and those who exaggerate their own worth.
The true lover rejects the gold because he knows the
difference between appearance and reality, and he rejects
the silver because he knows he does not deserve Portia.
The dialogue between Portia and Bassanio before he
makes his choice informs him that Portia wants him
to choose aright and, therefore, that she loves him; and
Portia becomes convinced that he loves her, rather than
her fortune. He therefore knows that he is hazarding
all he has in submitting to the test of the caskets; and
this is why the motto on the leaden casket appeals to
him.

The two main plots of the play are linked by the
fact that both are concerned with the falsity of money
values—the blood in the veins of Bassanio and Antonio is contrasted with Shylock's wealth—and it is
poetically fitting that the Jew should be foiled by the
quibble about a drop of blood. The worlds of Venice
and Belmont are contrasted, the one concerned with

commerce and the other with love and music. The third contrast in the play, apparent in the trial scene, is between the Old Testament and the New.

In some performances of the play, the part of Shylock is sentimentalized so that his defeat is treated almost tragically. To an Elizabethan audience, however, he would seem to have been treated mercifully: his life was spared, he was not deprived of all his property, and his forcible conversion would enable him to escape the fires of hell. Portia gives him every opportunity to act mercifully; and it is his insistence on the letter of the law that brings about his well-merited defeat and punishment.

In the next comedy, *Much Ado About Nothing,* the villain who slanders Hero is a minor character; and we know both from the title of the play and from the fact that Borachio has been arrested before Hero's rejection in church that all will come right in the end. There are two plots, and they are neatly woven together by the fact that the uniting of Beatrice and Benedick is a game played to occupy the time before Hero's marriage, by the theme, common to both, of the power of rumor, of overhearing, of which there are six examples in the course of the play, and by the iterative imagery concerned with clothing or disguise, which exemplify the contrast between appearance and reality—the seeming unchastity of Hero and the seeming hatred of Benedick and Beatrice for each other.

Benedick and Beatrice are, of course, in love from the start: their sparring is a sign of their mutual attraction. But Beatrice exercises her wit at Benedick's expense because she thinks he had been philandering with her; and they are both in reaction against marriages of convenience and against the sentimentalities of romantic love.

To a modern audience Claudio's rejection of Hero at the altar, a scene invented by Shakespeare, is apt to seem unpardonable. But it must be remembered that it was a recognized convention in Elizabethan drama that the hero should believe in the villain's slander of the heroine. Without this convention Beatrice's faith in her cousin would seem to be merely the natural behavior of an ordinary decent person instead of a faith against all reason and a genuine proof of the loyalty of her heart.

As You Like It, based on *Rosalynde*, is the first of Shakespeare's comedies for which he went to an English novel. But he does not merely dramatize this pastoral romance: he uses it in such a way as to produce a satire on pastoralism, and hence a comedy of love. In so doing he links several different conventions. There is first the convention of the noble outlaw, with its pretense, exposed by Jaques, that life under the greenwood tree is preferable to life at court. But Jaques' melancholy is attacked by the exiled Duke on the grounds that it is a result of his youthful profligacy and by Rosalind for its affectation. Second, there is the pastoral convention, going back to Theocritus and Virgil, of a lovesick swain enamored of a cruel shepherdess. Rosalind disposes of this when she attacks the scornful Phoebe. Third, Rosalind and Celia are aristocrats who play at being a shepherd and shepherdess. Fourth, we have a picture of country people as imagined by the town: William and Audrey, typical country bumpkins, are satirized by Touchstone. Last, in the shape of Corin we have a portrait of an almost Wordsworthian shepherd.

There is a great deal of cross-satire in the play. Touchstone satirizes everyone; Jaques satirizes the Duke and Orlando; and Rosalind satirizes not only Jaques and Phoebe, but the whole conception of romantic love. But in spite of her mockery of the idea that rejected lovers die—"men have died from time to time and worms have eaten them, but not for love"—Rosalind herself is fathoms deep in love. By mocking the conventions and illusions of love, Shakespeare is rescuing it from the fashionable counterfeits and distortions of his age. "True love undergoes the refining process of satire, and survives in a less questionable and ambiguous form."

Twelfth Night was based mainly on a tale in Barnabe Rich's *Farewell to Military Profession,* but there is some evidence to show that Shakespeare was acquainted with one or more Italian plays on a similar theme. Leslie Hotson has argued that the incident where Malvolio interrupts the revelers was based on a topical story of how Sir William Knollys, Comptroller of the Household, had broken up a noisy party in the palace in the small hours of the morning. But Dr. Hotson's main theory about the play, that it was written and rehearsed in ten days so as to be performed before Virginio Orsino, Duke of Bracciano, when he was visiting the English court, is less likely—not because Shakespeare could not have written his most polished comedy in so short a time but because the portrait of Orsino in the play is by no means a flattering one. He is satirized for his sentimental love-melancholy. Nor would Queen Elizabeth have liked to see herself in the character of Olivia, the girl who is satirized for her sentimental love for her dead brother, whom she proposes with exquisite absurdity to lament for seven years:

> And water once a day her chamber round
> With eye-offending brine.

The play is, in fact, a satire on different kinds of sentimentality, though its victims are cured before the end of the play: Orsino is cured of his sentimental love for a woman he hardly knows by a more genuine love for Viola; Olivia is cured of her affected attachment to her dead brother by a genuine passion for Cesario; Sir Andrew is cured by the emptiness of his purse; and Malvolio is cured of his ambitious fantasies by resentment.

Malvolio, like Shylock, is sometimes sentimentalized in performance. It should be remembered that he is egotistical, censorious, and (as Olivia remarks) sick of self-love. He is snared by the forged letter only because he has had daydreams of "having come from a day bed where I have left Olivia sleeping." His bitter remarks about Feste and his interruption of the party justify (in the world of the play) the trick that is played on him. "Dost thou think because thou art virtuous there shall be no more cakes and ale?" inquires Sir Toby. But Malvolio is self-righteous rather than virtuous.

The most attractive scenes in the two previous comedies—between Beatrice and Benedick and between Rosalind and Orlando—had been in prose. There is plenty of racy prose in *Twelfth Night,* notably in the Sir Toby and Malvolio scenes, but Orlando, Olivia, and Viola speak mainly in verse. At its best, as in the scene where "Come away, Death" is sung and Viola teaches Orsino his first lesson in the meaning of love, it is incomparably beautiful. The whole play, indeed, is steeped in lyrical beauty so that even the most farcial scenes are never merely funny. Plotting, characterization, atmosphere, and poetry all exhibit Shakespeare at the height of his powers as a writer of comedy; and its very perfection may have turned him to experiment in other kinds.

It has often been pointed out that in these four central comedies the heroines best embody their spirit and that the heroes are comparatively colorless beside them. All four are gallant, resourceful, witty, generous, and loving; but no one would mistake a speech of Rosalind's for one of Beatrice's, or one of Portia's for one of Viola's.

One other characteristic of Shakespearian comedy may be mentioned: it has been fruitfully analyzed by Professor B. Evans. Shakespeare never keeps his audience in the dark, except letting them believe that Hermione is dead in *The Winter's Tale*. We know that Cesario is Viola in disguise and that she has a twin brother; that Ganymede is Rosalind; that Portia is the learned doctor; and that Hero has been slandered.

Twelfth Night seems to have been sandwiched between two tragedies—*Julius Caesar* and *Hamlet*. Shakespeare had read North's translation of Plutarch's *Lives* in 1595; but five years elapsed before he dramatized the assassination of Julius Caesar. There were two attitudes toward the assassination in Shakespeare's day: that the murder of the greatest man who ever lived was the worst of crimes and that Brutus attempted to save the Roman Republic by a noble act of tyrannicide. Some critics believe that Brutus in Shakespeare's play was tempted into murdering a great man by the envious Cassius, and others think that Shakespeare depicted Caesar as a tyrant who was rightly slain. Confronted with these opposing views, E. Schanzer has argued that Shakespeare was deliberately ambiguous. After hearing some of Caesar's speeches, we are left wondering if Caesar is a great man or the mere shell of former greatness. Brutus, "the noblest Roman of them all," has many attractive traits: his love of his wife, his solicitude for Lucius, his obvious integrity. But there are many speeches and incidents that give us a very different impression of his character and make us think that he is vain, self-righteous, mistaken in his practical judgments, and given to self-deception. He boasts too much of his own integrity. He wants Cassius to raise money by the "vile means" he is too dainty to use himself. He pretends that he has not heard of Portia's death so that he can show off his stoicism. In the most revealing speech of all—the one in which he makes up his mind to murder Caesar—he admits that Caesar has not proved to be a tyrant, but that if he is crowned he may become one. This not only ignores the fact that Caesar has refused the crown and that he already has absolute power: it slips in the monstrous assumption that it is legitimate to kill a man for crimes he has not yet committed. Another example of Brutus' self-deception is in his wish to kill the spirit of Caesar without killing Julius the man; and he wants the killing to be a sacrifice and not a hunt or butchery. After the murder it is clear that the conspirators have killed the man but not Caesarism, and Antony calls them butchers and hunters.

Shakespeare learned a great deal from Plutarch, and **the play** is a wonderful evocation of the last days of the

Republic. He uses supernatural portents to create an atmosphere of foreboding and terror. "The heavens themselves blaze forth the death of princes." The first three acts of the play are some of the most exciting that Shakespeare ever wrote; and if in the last two acts the tension is slackened, they too contain some magnificent scenes, including that of the quarrel and reconciliation of Brutus and Cassius.

If there is controversy about *Julius Caesar* because Brutus is given few moments of direct self-revelation, there is even greater controversy about *Hamlet,* despite the prolonged introspection of the hero. Shakespeare took his plot from a popular old play in which the hero is given the task of avenging his father's murder on his uncle, without harming his mother, who is married to the murderer. Hamlet receives the ghost's command before the end of Act I; and he succeeds in his mission at the end of the play, only after the deaths of Polonius (killed in mistake for the King), Ophelia (driven mad by her father's death), Rosencrantz and Guildenstern (killed by Hamlet in self-defense), Gertrude (who drinks the poisoned wine intended for Hamlet), and Laertes (killed by his own poisoned rapier).

Many explanations have been offered for Hamlet's delay: melancholy, weakness of will, "losing the power of action in the energy of resolve," Oedipus complex, a half-conscious revolt against the morality of revenge, to mention a few. There has, perhaps, in the criticism of *Hamlet* during the past 150 years, been too much concentration on the psychology of the hero and too little on the objective situation in which he is placed. Although he believes in the genuineness of the ghost, he cannot kill Claudius without further evidence of his guilt. He feigns madness to cover up the shock he has received and so puts Claudius on his guard; thus, he is trying to obtain proof of his uncle's guilt at the same time as his uncle is trying to discover the cause of his madness. He obtains the necessary proof at the performance of "The Mousetrap," but by his behavior lets Claudius know that he knows. From that moment it is obvious that if he does not kill Claudius, Claudius will kill him. Immediately afterward he discovers the King at his prayers; and either because he wants to ensure his damnation or, as some think, because he cannot kill a defenseless man, he lets the opportunity slip. A few minutes later he kills the eavesdropper behind the arras, believing him to be the King. Thereafter he has no further chance of killing Claudius until he himself is dying from the poisoned rapier; but in the last act, after his return from England, he believes that his providential escape on the pirate ship is a sign that God will provide him with a suitable opportunity of executing justice. This contrasts with his agonizing attempts in his previous soliloquies to discover the causes of his failure:

> Bestial oblivion or some craven scruple
> Of thinking too precisely on the event.

The long and exciting struggle between Hamlet and his uncle, which leads to the death of both at almost the same moment, is underlined by the imagery derived from war. This is in quantity and quality as significant as the famous sickness imagery that is designed to depict the rottenness of the court and the corruption that springs from the unpunished murder of the late King. This does not mean that Hamlet is unflawed. Shakespeare had read Timothy Bright's *Treatise of Melancholy,* and Hamlet is depicted as a man who is seriously unbalanced by his mother's frailty. Later, his disgust at his own impotence leads him to several outbursts of hysterical violence; his treatment of Ophelia exhibits the cruelty of a disappointed idealist; and he is callous in his remarks about some of his victims. Hamlet is, in fact, infected with the evil he seeks to root out; but this is an occupational disease of avengers in Elizabethan plays.

The other thing that needs to be stressed is the way Hamlet is contrasted with other characters. There are four avengers in the play. Laertes is anxious to avenge the deaths of Polonius and Ophelia; and his unscrupulousness is contrasted with Hamlet's more civilized vacillation. He is prepared to cut Hamlet's throat in church; he anoints his rapier with the poison he bought for such emergencies. Those critics who complain of Hamlet's delay should consider whether they really prefer Laertes. The second avenger is Fortinbras, described by Hamlet as "a delicate and tender prince," but one who is prepared to lead thousands of men to their deaths in an unjust war, "for a fantasy and trick of fame." Pyrrhus, in the Dido play, is a ruthless king-killer. These three characters are introduced into the play as a means of demonstrating Hamlet's more civilized and sensitive demeanor, even though he himself uses them as a spur to his "dull revenge."

Hamlet is also contrasted with Horatio, the man who has borne with equal thanks the buffets and rewards of fortune, one who is not

> a pipe for Fortune's finger
> To sound what stop she please.

Hamlet, here and elsewhere, is filled with self-reproaches, unaware of his subconscious reluctance to perform what he regards as a solemn duty. But Horatio would presumably have decided to suffer

The slings and arrows of outrageous fortune

rather than to kill the murderer of his father; and this was not a course that Hamlet could properly adopt.

Some critics, faced with the contradictory interpretations of their predecessors, have maintained that Hamlet is Everyman rather than a particular character. Others, with greater plausibility, have argued that Shakespeare took over from his source play incidents that he failed to harmonize with the sophisticated figure he created. But it is more profitable to suppose that Shakespeare deliberately placed a man such as Hamlet—intelligent, sensitive, and civilized—in a situation where his very virtues became liabilities. The most successful dramatic characters are those that cannot easily be described. The reality of Hamlet depends on the inconsistencies, the discrepancies, the imperfect self-knowledge, the unexplained motives, the mystery of human personality embodied in the parable of the recorders, which is given a central place in the play. If Hamlet were unreal, we should not have had so much controversy about him.

Hamlet was written in the last years of Queen Elizabeth's reign. The other great tragedies belong to the reign of her successor. But before the Queen died in 1603, Shakespeare seems to have written one more play, *Troilus and Cressida,* in some ways the most enigmatic of all his works. It was written, apparently, for a private performance at one of the Inns of Court and afterward revised. A number of recent critics have argued that it belongs to the genre of "comical satire" popular at the beginning of the seventeenth century, to which Jonson, Marston, and Dekker all contributed. The play certainly contains some satire. It has been suspected that Thersites and Ajax were intended to be satirical portraits of Marston and Jonson; and even if this is dubious, there is no doubt that the Greeks in the play are all presented in a satirical light. Just as the war plot is accompanied by the scurrilous invective of Thersites, so the love plot is accompanied by the sentimental obscenities of Pandarus. But although the play contains some satirical and some farcical comedy, it is difficult to regard "comical satire" as an appropriate label. The full-scale debates in the Greek camp and in the Trojan council of war, the disillusionment of Troilus, and the murder of Hector are not presented satirically. Nor is it possible to agree with those critics who pretend that Troilus is a sexually sophisticated Italianate roué. The point of the scene in which Troilus and Cressida vow eternal faithfulness is that Troilus is a traditionally faithful lover, Cressida traditionally faithless, and Pandarus the traditional go-between. Troilus' naïve idealism and immaturity is equally apparent in the debate in Troy.

What Shakespeare seems to be doing is taking the two subjects that men have always tended to idealize—war and sex—and showing the reality. Instead of the Homeric glamour surrounding the Trojan War, we are told that "all the argument is a whore and a cuckold." Helen is a sentimental fool; Achilles is a surly bully; Agamemnon a windbag; Ulysses a Machiavellian "politician."

In spite of his use of Pandarus as a go-between and

in spite of his doubts about Cressida, which are shown by his reiterated prayer that she should be true, Troilus idealizes the shallow woman he loves and desires. When he watches her unfaithfulness the bottom drops out of his universe. His disillusionment is essentially tragic; and the murder of Hector, the one character who retains his classical nobility, is used to show how chivalry is incompatible with the harsh realities of war.

Nineteenth-century critics found the play cynical and suggested that Shakespeare was passing through a period of disgust with sex. But he had recently depicted Rosalind and Viola, and he was about to create Desdemona. Any dramatist who chose to write on the subject of Cressida would be acquainted not merely with Chaucer's great poem but also with Henryson's sequel, *The Testament of Cresseid,* in which Cressida, after becoming a harlot, is afflicted with leprosy; and the name of the genial Pandarus of Chaucer's poem had become the generic term for a pimp. The general atmosphere of the play thus reflects the literary tradition rather than Shakespeare's personal feelings; and even the unflattering portraits of the Homeric heroes may be traced to the Virgilian tradition and to the belief that the Trojans landed in Britain.

By 1603 Shakespeare had completed his main series of histories, and they show a continuous improvement and a growing maturity. He had written his major comedies, and he was just entering the period of the great tragedies. If he had died in the same year as the Queen, he would still have been the best English dramatist, although his greatest plays were still to come. But it is important to recognize how much he owed to his predecessors: Kyd, Marlowe, Lyly, and Greene; how much he owed to the conditions of the Elizabethan stage and to the stimulus of his audience, not least of the groundlings; and how much his achievement depended on the great output of works in prose and verse during the last fifteen years of the great Queen's reign.

Suggested Reading

Biographies of Shakespeare include: *Shakespeare, Truth and Tradition* by J. S. Smart (Oxford: Clarendon Press, 1928); *The Life of Shakespeare* by F. E. Halliday (London: Duckworth, 1961); *William Shakespeare* by A. L. Rowse (London: Macmillan, 1964); and *Shakespeare* by Peter Quennell (London: Weidenfeld and Nicolson, 1964). Most of the basic facts are included in *Shakespeare: Facts and Problems* by E. K. Chambers (Oxford: Clarendon Press, 1930). A few more were added by L. Hotson in *Shakespeare Versus Shallow* (London: Nonesuch, 1931) and *I, William Shakespeare* (London: Cape, 1937).

Shakespeare's Life and Art by P. Alexander (London: Nisbet, 1938) and *Shakespeare* by H. Fluchère (London: Longmans, 1953) are valuable introductions. There are up-to-date bibliographies in *Shakespeare, The Writer and His Work*, edited by B. Dobrée (London: Longmans, 1964). The best work on Shakespeare as a dramatist is *Prefaces to Shakespeare* by H. Granville-Barker (Princeton Univ. Press, 1946).

Narrative and Dramatic Sources of Shakespeare have been collected by G. Bullough (New York: Columbia Univ. Press, 1957–) and discussed in *Shakespeare's Sources I* by Kenneth Muir (London: Methuen, 1957). *Shakespeare's Plutarch*, edited by T. J. B. Spencer (Harmondsworth: Penguin Books, 1964) is convenient and inexpensive.

The best one-volume text is probably P. Alexander's (London and Glasgow: Collins, 1951). Annotated editions include the new "Cambridge," edited by Q. and J. D. Wilson (Cambridge Univ. Press; 1920–   ); Kittredge's (Boston: Ginn, 1939–   ); the new Arden (Cambridge, Mass.: Harvard Univ. Press, 1951) with fuller notes; Signet (New York: New American Library, 1963–   ) containing essays on each play; and Pelican (Baltimore: Penguin Books, 1956–   ). The first twelve volumes of a new British Penguin edition are appearing in 1967.

Books on the comedies include *Shakespearian Comedy* by H. B. Charlton (London: Methuen, 1938); *Shakespeare's Comedies* by B. Evans (Oxford Univ. Press, 1960); *Shakespeare and His Comedies* by J. R. Brown (London: Methuen, 1957); and *Shakespeare: The Comedies,* edited by Kenneth Muir (Englewood Cliffs, N. J.: Prentice-Hall, 1965).

Books on the histories include *Shakespeare's History Plays* by E. M. W. Tillyard (London: Chatto and Windus, 1944); *Shakespeare's Histories* by L. B. Campbell (San Marino: Huntington Library, 1947); *The Cease of Majesty* by M. M. Reese (London: Arnold, 1961); *Shakespeare: The Histories,* edited by E. M. Waith (Englewood Cliffs, N. J.: Prentice-Hall, 1965); *Shakespeare from Richard II to Henry V* by D. Traversi (London: Hollis and Carter, 1958); and *Shakespeare's Histories* by A. C. Sprague (London: The Society for Theatre Research, 1964). See also *The Fortunes of Falstaff* by J. D. Wilson (Cambridge Univ. Press, 1943).

Books on the tragedies include *Shakespearean Tragedy* by A. C. Bradley (London: Macmillan, 1904); *The Wheel of Fire* (Oxford Univ. Press, 1930) and *The Imperial Theme* (Oxford Univ. Press, 1931) by G. Wilson Knight; *Shakespeare: The Tragedies,* edited by A. Harbage (Englewood Cliffs, N. J.: Prentice-Hall, 1965). *Julius Caesar* is discussed in *The Problem Plays of Shakespeare* by E. Schanzer (London: Routledge and Kegan Paul, 1963) and *The Structure of Julius Caesar* by A. Bonjour (Liverpool Univ. Press, 1958). Of the scores of books on *Hamlet* the following may be mentioned:

What Happens in Hamlet by J. D. Wilson (Cambridge Univ. Press, 1935).

Hamlet Father and Son by P. Alexander (Oxford: Clarendon Press, 1955).

The Question of Hamlet by H. Levin (New York: The Viking Press, 1959).

Hamlet, edited by J. R. Brown and B. Harris (London: Arnold, 1963).

Shakespeare: Hamlet by Kenneth Muir (London: Arnold, 1963).

Selective Bibliography

ANTHOLOGIES

Ault, N., *Elizabethan Lyrics* (London: Longmans, 1925).

Chambers, E. K., *The Oxford Book of Sixteenth Century Verse* (Oxford: Clarendon Press, 1932).

Donno, E. S., *Elizabethan Minor Epics* (London: Routledge and Kegan Paul, 1963).

Hebel, J. W., and others, *Tudor Poetry and Prose* (New York: Appleton-Century-Crofts, 1953).

Lamson, R., and H. Smith, *Renaissance England* (New York: Norton, 1956).

McClure, N. E., *Sixteenth Century English Poets* (New York: Harper, 1954).

Muir, Kenneth, *Elizabethan Lyrics* (London: Harrap, 1952).

CRITICISM

Baker, H., *Induction to Tragedy* (Louisiana State Univ. Press, 1939).

Bevington, D. M., *From "Mankind" to Marlowe* (Cambridge, Mass.: Harvard Univ. Press, 1962).

Bradbrok, M. C., *Themes and Conventions of Elizabethan Tragedy* (Cambridge Univ. Press, 1935).

———, *The Growth and Structure of Elizabethan Comedy* (London: Chatto and Windus, 1955).

Brown, J. R., and B. Harris, eds., *Elizabethan Theatre* (London: Arnold, 1966).

Doran, M., *Endeavors of Art* (Madison: Univ. of Wisconsin Press, 1954).

Ing, C., *Elizabethan Lyrics* (London: Chatto and Windus, 1951).

Joseph, Sister M., *Rhetoric in Shakespeare's Time* (New York: Harcourt, Brace & World, 1962).

Lever, J. W., *The Elizabethan Love Sonnet* (London: Methuen, 1956).

Lewis, C. S., *English Literature in the Sixteenth Century* (Oxford: Clarendon Press, 1954).

Pattison, B., *Music and Poetry of the English Renaissance* (London: Methuen, 1948).

Smith, H., *Elizabethan Poetry* (Cambridge, Mass.: Harvard Univ. Press, 1952).

Tillyard, E. M. W., *The Elizabethan World Picture* (London: Chatto and Windus, 1943).

Tuve, R., *Elizabethan and Metaphysical Imagery* (Univ. of Chicago Press, 1946).

Wilson, F. P., *Elizabethan and Jacobean* (Oxford: Clarendon Press, 1945).

Index

ABOUT THE AUTHOR

KENNETH MUIR is King Alfred Professor of English Literature at the University of Liverpool, where he has taught since 1951. A noted authority on Shakespeare and Wyatt, Professor Muir has been a frequent lecturer at universities in the United States and throughout Europe, and in 1957 he was a Fellow at the Folger Shakespeare Library. His publications are too numerous to list here in their entirety, but among them are *Shakespeare's Sources* (1957), *Shakespeare as Collaborator* (1960), and *Last Periods of Shakespeare, Racine, and Ibsen* (1961). Among his many editions are *Macbeth* (1951), *King Lear* (1952), *Elizabethan Lyrics* (1952), *John Keats: A Reassessment* (1958), *Shakespeare: Comedies* (1965), and *Othello* (1967).